New Directions in Theology Today

VOLUME III
God and Secularity

New Directions in Theology Today
WILLIAM HORDERN, GENERAL EDITOR

VOL. I INTRODUCTION
BY WILLIAM HORDERN

VOL. II HISTORY AND HERMENEUTICS
BY CARL E. BRAATEN

VOL. III GOD AND SECULARITY
BY JOHN MACQUARRIE

VOL. IV THE CHURCH
BY COLIN WILLIAMS

VOL. V CHRISTIAN LIFE
BY PAUL HESSERT

VOL. VI MAN
BY ROGER L. SHINN

VOL. VII CHRIST
BY ROBERT CLYDE JOHNSON

NEW DIRECTIONS IN THEOLOGY TODAY

Volume III
God
and
Secularity

BY
JOHN MACQUARRIE

Lutterworth Press
London

First published 1968

COPYRIGHT © MCMLXVI W. L. JENKINS

PRINTED IN THE UNITED STATES OF AMERICA

TO
ARTHUR AND NETTIE McNAUGHTAN

Editor's Foreword

Theology always has existed in some tension with the church. But there is considerable evidence that today the gulf is wider than ever before. To both pastors and laymen, it often seems that contemporary theology is working in opposition to the concerns of the parish. They are disturbed to read in newspapers and popular journals about theologians who seem to have lightly cast aside the cornerstones of the faith and who argue that the parish is doomed. To the theologian the parish often appears to be a respectable club dedicated to erecting buildings, raising budgets, and avoiding controversial issues.

There is little active dialogue between the theologian and the church today. The fault for this lies with both parties, but the situation is becoming increasingly serious as the church moves into a new age. This series is dedicated to the task of bridging the present gulf.

One of the reasons for the gulf between theology and the church is that neither the busy pastor nor the concerned layman can keep up to date with an ever-expanding theological literature. Thus, the purpose of New Directions in Theology Today is to present concise summaries of the present scene in theology. The series is not for the lazy pastor, nor for the layman who is beginning his theological education. Rather, these volumes are especially prepared for the busy pastor who is concerned with keeping abreast of modern theology and for the layman who, having been initiated into theology, is reading for further study, particularly to find out what contemporary Christian thinkers are saying.

The series is not written with the assumption that only professional theologians have something to say, but is offered in the hope that it will stimulate pastors and laymen to enter into the theological dialogue, and with the conviction that a vital theology for our time must be the work of the church as a whole.

WILLIAM HORDERN

Contents

Preface

Of all the questions that are being debated in the so-called "new theology," surely the question of God has a central place. Belief in God seems to lie at the foundation of Christian and Biblical faith. But how can this belief be maintained or even understood in a secularized world that seems to be able to get along very well in many ways without God?

This book offers a report on the recent and current debates about God, analyzes and criticizes some of the views that have been put forward, and indicates the directions in which, as the author believes, theology can move if there is to be some hope of resolving the present problems.

Whatever the outcome of the debates over God may be, it is surely a gain that Christian theologians are probing the foundations of their faith with such freedom and openness. Too often theology has been sidetracked into the discussion of peripheral issues, and we must be glad that its attention is now focused on fundamental questions.

The title of this book is meant to indicate the two poles between which the current theological discussions move. This title, "God and Secularity," was used by me for an extended article published in seven installments in *The Holy Cross Magazine*, Vol. LXXVII, March to September issues, 1966. Some of the material from this series has been incorporated, in a revised and enlarged form, into the present book, and I wish to thank the Father Superior of the Order of the Holy Cross for permission to make use of the material in this way.

In Chapter VIII, I have used material from a paper on "Divine Omnipotence," prepared for the Seventh Inter-American Congress of Philosophy, held at Laval University, Quebec, in 1967.

The annotated book list in the Appendix was first prepared as a reading guide for pastors in the continuing education program at Union Theological Seminary. The list has now been expanded and brought up to date.

J. M.

Union Theological Seminary
New York City

CHAPTER I

The Poles of the Discussion

God and secularity: these are the poles between which the contemporary theological discussion moves, and at first sight they seem to be poles that are infinitely apart.

One pole is constituted by God. Theology cannot fail to talk of God, for the very word "theology" means "God talk." Let us be quite clear at the outset that if anyone wants to construct a theology without God, he is pursuing a self-contradictory notion and is confusing both himself and other people. He may construct a philosophy of religion (and he may even do this brilliantly), or he may construct a doctrine of man (anthropology) or a doctrine of Jesus (Jesusology) or an ethic or a mixture of all of these, but whatever results from his endeavors, it will not be a theology.

The other pole of the discussion is constituted by secularity. Nowadays theology has to be done in a secularized world. If the theologian cannot avoid the responsibility of speaking of God, it is equally true that he cannot avoid the responsibility of addressing himself to his own world and of speaking the language of his time. But is not a secularized world precisely a world without God, a world in which God has become an unnecessary hypothesis? Is not, then, theology torn apart and destroyed as it tries to span the poles between which its discussion must nowadays move? Does this not mean in turn that we should indeed abandon theology, and do so quite explicitly? We might substitute for it an ethic or a doctrine of man or whatever would be considered appropriate—perhaps even a Jesus-ology of some sort, if a sufficient number of people still have a nostalgic affection for the Christian faith and want to keep a place for Jesus somewhere.

I have asserted quite bluntly that theology cannot fail to talk of God. Perhaps there are some Christian doctrines so peripheral that we could, if necessary, get along without them. There are probably very few such doctrines, for the Christian faith has developed as a unity, and even doctrines that seem peripheral may make their contribution to the understanding of the whole, if we interpret them rightly and see them in the context of the whole. Yet, supposing we were to allow that some doctrines might be dispensable, we could never reckon the doctrine of God among them. This doctrine has a central place and is presupposed in all the others. The reader may remember Rudyard Kipling's poem about Gunga Din, a water carrier in the British Army in India, whose name was constantly on the lips of the soldiers, day in, day out: "It was 'Din! Din! Din!'" We might say that in the Bible, in the liturgy, in the creeds and confessions of the church, it is "God! God! God!" Wherever we turn, we hear his name.

"In the beginning God created the heavens and the earth." (Gen. 1:1.) The Old Testament goes on to unfold the theme of God as the ruler, the judge, and the hope of history, the One with reference to whom all things are to be interpreted. When the New Testament sets forth Jesus Christ, it must confess with Paul: "All this is from God.

. . . God was in Christ" (II Cor. 5:18–19). When Christians came to draw up a formal creed, it could hardly begin otherwise than: "I believe in God. . . ."

If one were to try to eliminate all this talk of God, I do not know what would be left, but surely it would be something quite different from the faith of the Bible and the church. Schubert Ogden expresses the matter truly and forthrightly when he declares: "However absurd talking about God might be, it could never be so obviously absurd as talking of Christian faith without God."[1]

Yet it must be acknowledged that the word "God" has become a very elusive one. It is possible that talking about God just is absurd and that all theology is absurd too. What do we mean by this word "God"? Or what do we mean by saying that we believe in God? Is not our world, as we understand it and manage it nowadays, complete in itself without God?

It is surely true that in the busy world of today we can live for most of the time on the level of the "everyday"— the level of limited problems, limited goals, limited enjoyments, all capable of being handled without any thought of God. Yet, as I have tried to show elsewhere,[2] there are times (perhaps in the lives of all of us) when we are jolted out of the "everyday" and compelled to ask questions that range farther afield. These questions, of course, are there all the time. They underlie our everyday activities, and we have already assumed some answers to them; yet perhaps only rarely do these questions get explicitly asked. They are questions about our own being, our actions, values, goals; but since man's being cannot be considered in isolation, these questions have a way of broadening out, so that we ask about that wider context in which human life is set. It is along this way that we come at last to the question of God, whether or not we explicitly recognize the question as such. Even if we never consciously do metaphysics or ontology, and even if we declare our contempt for such exercises, the very policies and stances that we adopt disclose some ontological convictions. I use the word "ontology" here in its widest sense for our beliefs about the way things are, about what is ultimately real and important.

Harvey Cox has claimed that we are presently in transition from an ontological phase of human thinking to a functional phase.[3] If by this he means (and sometimes this does seem to be his meaning) that the old-fashioned metaphysics of substance and essences is being replaced by more dynamic concepts, he is undoubtedly correct and this transition has been going on for a long time. But at other times (noticeably in his attack on Tillich) he seems to mean that people now get along without any ontology at all, and about this he is certainly wrong. Even the positivist has an ontology of sorts, and so has the pragmatist, as William James was ready to admit. But Cox is no positivist, for he believes in a God who is active in history and urges us to cooperate with him. Such a God constitutes just as much of an ontological problem as the substantial God of traditional metaphysics. Hence James Alfred Martin, writing from the standpoint of analytical philosophy, has rightly indicated[4] that Cox has plenty of ontological convictions of his own. "How," asks Martin, "would one go about 'exploring the notions of teamwork and partnership . . . in our conceptualization of God' without ultimately considering the cosmic implications and foundations of these categories?" In Martin's view, Cox's position "bristles with unspecified and hence unexamined metaphysical assumptions of its own."

The Bishop of Woolwich, John A. T. Robinson, quotes

with approval a passage in which we are told that the old question, "How can I find a gracious God?" has been replaced by a new question, "How can I find a gracious neighbor?"[5] In a superficial way, this statement is true. That is to say, it is true so long as we remain on the level of the everyday, and it is true also, as a matter of fact, that the theological questions eagerly debated at the time of the Reformation have long since been forgotten. But one would need to be very much of a cynic to doubt the existence of the gracious neighbor. I did not serve very long in the British Army before I discovered that the "gracious neighbor" is met much oftener than theologians allow. The gracious neighbor keeps coming along, even when least expected—and, as often as not, he is not a Christian! No, the question that still disturbs us and that lies not very far below the surface is the old one about the gracious God, though possibly we do not formulate it that way anymore. It is the question of whether all the love and sacrifice and effort of a billion gracious neighbors really count and really achieve, or whether they are all doomed to frustration as so many useless passions in an essentially absurd (godless) world.

Incidentally, one would have supposed that the Bishop, of all men, would have been aware that the question of God is not so far away, even in the contemporary world. How else did *Honest to God* sell something like a million copies? It must have offered an answer to some question that people were asking, or it must have awakened some question that was only lightly slumbering. I think that Paul's words about God are still true: "He is not far from each one of us"; and Paul's reason for saying this still holds: For "in him we live and move and have our being" (Acts 17:27–28).

I myself should have thought that the decade before

World War II was much more positivistically-minded than the period in which we are now living—a period in which many serious-minded and intelligent people do find themselves asking questions that go far beyond pragmatic considerations and raise issues of ulterior, if not of ultimate, meaning and value. This is reflected in the career of recent philosophy itself, for it has moved from the logical positivism of a generation ago to the much more open and questioning attitude of today's analytic philosophy; and from the humanistic existentialism of the earlier part of the century to a more ontological type. Perhaps the trouble with some of our "new theologians" is the same trouble that theologians have often had—they are responding to the situation of the previous generation.

At any rate, not only *Honest to God* but a whole stream of books about God keep flowing from the press, and these books are being eagerly read by surprisingly large numbers of people, many of them outside the church. Oddly enough, this theme of God is a best-selling line, so it looks as if someone must be interested. In the years immediately after the publication of *Honest to God,* an amazing number of books about God have appeared, some of them quite unconnected with Bishop Robinson's venture. Let me list some of them: *The Problem of God: Yesterday and Today,* by John Courtney Murray, S.J.; *The Existence of God as Confessed by Faith,* by Helmut Gollwitzer; *The Search for God,* by Robert W. Gleason, S.J.; *The God We Seek,* by Paul Weiss; *The Real God,* by Alfred B. Starratt; *The Reality of God,* by Schubert M. Ogden; *Understanding God,* by Frederick Herzog; and, following a more negative line, *Radical Theology and the Death of God,* by Thomas J. J. Altizer and William Hamilton.[6] The stream shows no signs of drying up. The present author is even now adding another title to the list, and no doubt other writers are doing the same!

The simple fact that all these books about God are being written and read surely shows us that the question of God, even the explicit question, is still with us. Let us agree that the word "God" has become elusive and that the question of God is hard to formulate, so that people might find it difficult to say just what it is they are asking about. Yet, as I have claimed elsewhere, "in asking the question of God, man must already have some idea of God, for every question has its direction, and it is impossible to seek anything without having some understanding of what is sought, however vague and minimal that understanding may be."[7]

But now let us leave, for a time, the question of God and turn to the opposite pole of our discussion, secularity. This notion will demand a more extended consideration later,[8] but some preliminary remarks may be made now about the use of the notion in contemporary theology.

Certainly, one cannot read very far in contemporary theology without coming across the word "secular." It has become a new catchword, to be ranked with "kerygma," *Heilsgeschichte,* "demythologizing," and some of the other words that have dominated twentieth-century theological debates. We soon realize too that with many theologians, "secular" is no longer the bad word that it once was. The claims and achievements of the secular world are frankly recognized and positively evaluated, and this is a welcome change from some earlier theological denigrations of everything that was supposed to be "merely human."

So, concern with the problem of secularity has become a major preoccupation with many Christian writers. But this does not mean that there is any common mind on the subject, or even that there is any agreement as to what is meant by this word "secular." There is general agreement that the outlook of our age has become increasingly characterized by secularity (this is the process of "secularization"), and that the church must come to grips with this fact, in both its presentation and its practice of the Christian faith. But when it comes to spelling out how this is to be done, there are wide divergences of opinion. Some writers give a wholehearted and uncritical welcome to the secularization of our times and seem to think that what is required of the church is that it give up its judgmental attitudes of the past and simply conform (if it can!) to the demands of the secular mentality and ethos. But others are much more critical and cautious in their evaluation of the secular, and even if they are sympathetic to secular thought and achievement, they believe that Christianity gives the criterion by which the methods and goals of a secular civilization are to be measured. In other words, different writers are prepared to accept different degrees of secularization, and some are still resistant to the whole process; among all of them, there are differences as to the precise meaning to be attached to this word "secular."

Frequently, a distinction is made between "secularity" and "secularism," and, correspondingly, between the adjectives "secular" and "secularist." The distinction is, perhaps, a somewhat artificial one, and I doubt if it is found outside the writings of a few contemporary theologians. However, it is worth noting. "Secularity" is taken to mean the outlook characterized by the attitudes of modern science and, more generally, of this-worldly concerns. Such an outlook is almost universal in civilized countries. Those theologians who talk of "secularity" in this sense usually hold that it is possible to subscribe fully to this outlook and that it is not incompatible with belief in God. On the other hand, "secularism" is taken to mean the more rigid attitude of those who hold that *only* through science is any trustworthy knowledge to be attained and that *only* the tangible and human affairs of this world are worthy of attention. This attitude is usually criticized by those theologians who accept secularity, but some do not trouble with such fine distinctions and go all the way with secularism—though we have already seen reason to question whether, in such a case, they could still be reckoned theologians at all.

A brief consideration of four recent books will help to bring some of these differences into fuller view. All these books profess to deal with the question of Christianity and the secular. They show how wide is the range of opinions among those theologians who have turned their attention to the matter; and we shall see that each of them conceives of the secular differently.

The first book I shall mention is *The Secular Meaning of the Gospel*,[9] by Paul van Buren. This book seems to go just about as far as possible in capitulating to the demands of the secular. Basing his opinions mainly on the works of some positivist and empiricist British philosophers of recent decades, van Buren maintained that it has become impossible to believe in any reality apart from that which is open to the empirical investigation of the sciences. For him, therefore, the "secular" is understood as excluding any kind of transcendent reality.

Thus van Buren asked for what he called a "reduction" in Christian theology, so that its content might be brought entirely within the sphere of the secular. This "reduction" turns out to be a pretty severe mutilation of the traditional faith, for it means in effect that God himself is to be left out. Van Buren's views are to be counted as belonging to the school that is trying to reconstruct Christianity without God, though van Buren himself dislikes to be associated with such proclaimers of the "death of God" as Thomas J. J. Altizer and William Hamilton. Van Buren regards their writings as "journalistic," and certainly one would agree that his own version of "Christian atheism" is the most lucid and philosophical expression that this position has so far received. There is also an attractive honesty in his presentation. Even so, it is, perhaps, not a very consistent view that gets expounded.

In the somewhat shadowy Christianity that remains after the reduction to the dimensions of history and ethics, Christ is set forth as the paradigm of human existence, the man who attained a true freedom that he imparted to others. Since freedom is an extremely formal conception until we know what it is freedom for, or freedom from, the characterization of Jesus in terms of freedom is not very helpful. What is left still more obscure is the question of how this freedom of Jesus is imparted to the disciples. Van Buren says: "We might say that, on Easter, the freedom of Jesus began to be *contagious*."[10] What mysteries, psychological, theological, or even metaphysical, lie behind the allusion to Easter and the strange metaphor of "contagion" is a question left unanswered, but one cannot help wondering whether, at this point, van Buren is not breaking out from the self-imposed limits of his "reduced" theology. When he goes on to say that Jesus' freedom is "caught" by us as something that happens to us, rather than something that we choose, he seems to be speaking of something very like what is traditionally called "grace."

Actually, at the time when he wrote this book, van Buren did recognize a kind of residual value in some of the Christian doctrines, when drastically reinterpreted in accordance with his secular version of the gospel—and perhaps this would mean a reinterpretation in terms of psychology. Likewise, he seemed to recognize a certain value (presumably again psychological) in the practices of prayer and worship. But in an interview with Ved Mehta,[11] he subsequently made it clear that he had come to the point where he no longer attached value to prayer and no longer exercised his Christian ministry. Such consequences seem to follow inevitably from his book, unless he chose to develop in a more positive way that mystery of grace which seemed to be still left in the secular gospel and which we have noted above.

So in this first version of secular Christianity that we have examined, we seem to be left with no more than the exhortation to take Jesus as the paradigm of the good life. Van Buren's secularity (or secularism) has eliminated any notion of the transcendent. It might occur to us, however, that since Jesus himself lived out of the transcendent, and his whole existence was centered on the Father, he could hardly be a suitable paradigm for the secular man whom van Buren has in mind. One wonders what such a secularist would make of our Lord's saying: "Why do you call me good? No one is good but God alone" (Mark 10:18).

Let us now turn to another book, *Secular Christianity,* by Ronald Gregor Smith.[12] This book promises an account of Christianity that will be "thoroughly secular," but we soon find ourselves moving among ideas very different from those of van Buren. Whereas the latter had relied on British empirical philosophy and on logical analysis, Gregor Smith takes little note of these and is oriented instead to an existential understanding of history, and especially to Bultmann's interpretation of the New Testa-

ment in existential and historical terms. This is precisely
the interpretation that van Buren had rejected, in his criticism of the somewhat similar Bultmannian stance of
Ogden.[13]

Gregor Smith develops the Bultmannian position in a
clear and persuasive manner through the first two thirds
of his book. His account of Christian faith is "thoroughly
secular" in the sense that it exhibits the meaning of faith
within the framework of temporal and historical existence.
No more than Bultmann does Gregor Smith wish to dispense with the notion of transcendence, though this would
certainly be understood, not as some "timeless" or "supra-
historical" reality, but rather as a dimension in history
itself, so that God too is historical—or even, perhaps, God
is history.

It is not easy to see how the final part of Gregor Smith's
book coheres with the earlier parts. In this final part, he
turns to Gogarten and Bonhoeffer rather than to Bultmann, and the views of these scholars are not so easily
harmonized. Bonhoeffer in particular became very critical
not only of Bultmann but of the whole existentialist influence in the interpretation of Christian faith. But from our
point of view, the main interest in this final part of Gregor
Smith's book is his criticism of van Buren, bringing into
relief the differences between them with regard to their
ways of understanding the secular. Gregor Smith writes: "If
van Buren were as respectful towards the whole herme-
neutical debate concerning the history of Jesus, the nature
of the kerygma, and the form-critical issues, as he is
towards the analytic philosophers, he could never be content with this attenuated and undialectical summary."[14]
He is critical of van Buren's "Jesusology" and claims that
we must speak not only of Jesus but also of the transcen-

dent God who meets us in and through Jesus. We cannot, indeed, speak of God "in himself," but we can recognize his transcendence in the historical experiences of faith. So this kind of secularity, while it stresses the temporal and the historical, does not want to eliminate God and the transcendent.

We pass now to a third book, *The Secular City*, by Harvey Cox. Here we find still another point of view represented. Cox is much less philosophical than either van Buren or Gregor Smith. He shows no special interest in either empiricism or existentialism and lets his thought be guided by sociological rather than philosophical considerations. Perhaps Cox is the most "American" of all the Christian secularists and he exhibits all the attractiveness together with all the weaknesses of that Christian activism which has been so prominent in America since the time of the social gospel and earlier. Cox is determined to take the secular mood of our time seriously, but this determination is coupled with a passionate concern for Christian ethical values and also with a remarkable attachment to the categories of Biblical theology, which are to be taken seriously as well. Those who regard Cox as a neo-Barthian are not far wrong, though it is a strangely Pelagian kind of Barthianism that emerges.

Cox, following Gogarten and others, regards secularization as an implicate of Biblical faith and of the doctrine of creation. The God of the Bible (for Cox does not attempt to dispense with God) is the God who is at work in secular history, not a God in some fenced-off religious sphere. Hence we are to look for God and cooperate with him in secular history, and this means in the social and political ferments of our own time.

The book is marred by its intemperate attacks on views

different from the author's own, and sometimes not even properly understood by him. We refer especially to his attacks on "metaphysics" and "ontology," and we have already seen that he has a fairly definite metaphysic of his own.[15] Other weaknesses of the book are its dubious exercises in Biblical exegesis, its preoccupation with sociological rather than theological categories, and, above all, its uncritical admiration for the achievements of technology and for the mentality of the contemporary secular man. On this last point, one must contrast with Cox's view the much more sober and dialectical approach to the secular found in Gregor Smith. One suspects that Cox harbors the old illusion that the "American dream" and the Kingdom of God are pretty much one and the same.

Nevertheless, Cox is right in condemning romantic nostalgia for the past. The kind of world he portrays, whether we like it or not, is the kind in which a great many people will have to live and the kind in which Christianity will have to find expression. We are offered at least the possibility of a more constructive Christian approach to the secular than we found in van Buren. But in this third book, the secular is understood chiefly in terms of a way of life —the way that belongs to the urbanized technological societies of today's world. This understanding of secularity still allows for God and his action, though it must be acknowledged that the thought of God remains somewhat shadowy in Cox's writing, and God's role is decidedly obscure.

The last of the four books on secularity that I want to mention is Eric Mascall's *The Secularization of Christianity*.[16] Described as "an analysis and a critique," this book departs from all unthinking acceptance of secularization and introduces the note of judgment and evaluation in the light of the Christian revelation. One would have thought that this was surely essential to any presentation of the Christian position, but it is sadly lacking in both van Buren and Cox. It so happens that Mascall is a considerably more able and more learned theologian than most of those whom he criticizes (his shafts are directed chiefly against van Buren and Bishop Robinson), and so he is able to expose many of the excesses, inconsistencies, and superficialities that have been put forward by the apostles of secularity. He is especially successful in showing how vulnerable is Robinson's position, and how much harder the Bishop will need to think if he is to produce anything like a coherent statement of his views.

But although Mascall scores in many dialectical battles, he does not win the war. The value of his book is chiefly as "a bulwark against heresies," in the phrase of Athanasius, a warning against extravagances and inconsistencies. It does not achieve very much in the way of a constructive handling of the problem of secularity. Although Mascall begins by frankly recognizing that the abiding truths of Christianity need changing modes of expression if they are to address the successive generations of mankind, he makes little headway himself (at least, in this book) in suggesting positive ways whereby the Christian faith can be communicated to the secular mentality of today and its impact brought to bear on contemporary society. He shows too little sympathy and understanding for the so-called "secular" outlook. Thus one feels that his criticisms, though often logically sound and valuable in detail, do not really overcome the views that he attacks.

Nevertheless, Mascall makes some very good points, which we should bear in mind. He is probably right in diagnosing the current theological stress on the secular as a violent swing against the past generation's stress on transcendence, and especially against "the extreme revelationism and supernaturalism of the school of Barth, Brunner and Heim."[17] Surely he is also right in his conclusion that the deference which many theologians are showing to the secular is excessive: "There is no valid ground for the failure of nerve which has stampeded many contemporary theologians into a total intellectual capitulation to their secular environment."[18]

We now have before us a provisional account of the poles between which current theology moves—the need to talk of God on the one side, the secular world on the other. We have already glimpsed something of the complexities of this situation, the different stances that can be taken up within it, and the very different ways in which the word "secularity" gets interpreted and the theological task in a secular world gets envisaged.

Needless to say, this complex situation did not come about overnight. If we are to understand it better, we must look at some of the factors that have gone to constitute it. The next two chapters will, therefore, be devoted to a further analysis and exploration of the background or context of the current question of God. We shall examine first the background of the question in recent theology, and then, in a fuller way than we have done so far, the meaning of secularity and its relation to atheism.

Chapter II

The Theological Background

Even a few years ago there were probably not very many people who would have guessed that the doctrine of God would turn out to be the "hot issue" in theology that it has proved to be. Who could have foreseen that the question of God would again become a lively and widely discussed issue? or that some Christian thinkers would be proclaiming the "death of God"? Yet once the great debate about God had broken out, it could be seen to have a certain inevitability about it. In retrospect, this debate can be seen as the point of convergence of many different tendencies in the theological thought that preceded it. To fill in something of this background is the purpose of the present chapter. To attempt to do this fully would require a book in itself, and would demand that we delve far back into the past. Here we must confine ourselves to a summary treatment of some of the more relevant trends in the past few decades.

A good starting point for our discussion is Bishop Robinson's *Honest to God,* the book that more than any other triggered the present debate. This book has become something of a symbol—the symbol, shall we say, of the right to discuss and question in a frank and open way, within the church, the most central doctrines of our Christian faith. In the earlier part of his career, Robinson had worked mainly in such "safe" areas as Biblical theology and liturgics. I call these areas "safe" because one pursues them on the assumption that the Bible and the liturgy are validated by a God who communicates with us through them. As long ago as 1955, I mildly rebuked John Robinson (he was not a Bishop at that time) for his unwillingness to allow to secular philosophy a say in the interpretation of the Bible, and for his apparent lack of sympathy with the radical questions that Bultmann was directing to the New Testament.[1] But with *Honest to God,* all that changed. Now the Bishop was facing some of the most basic issues in the Christian faith and thinking aloud about them in a most provocative manner.

I mentioned a convergence of theological trends, and it is precisely this convergence which we find in *Honest to God*—perhaps this was the secret of its catalytic property. Three important theologians of the last generation stand behind Robinson and supply the inspiration for his reflections: Paul Tillich, chiefly on the problem of God in philosophical terms; Rudolf Bultmann, on the problem of Biblical interpretation; and Dietrich Bonhoeffer, both on God and on the nature of the church. Robinson apparently believes that his most original contribution to theology has been to bring together Tillich, Bultmann, and Bonhoeffer. This may be true, but we should understand that he does this only in an eclectic way—he juxtaposes them without making any new synthesis. Perhaps Karl Barth was being a bit harsh when he said that the Bishop had mixed three good German beers and produced a lot of froth! But the fact remains that these three thinkers are brought together only superficially. It is even harder to imagine how one might combine Tillich and

Bonhoeffer than it is to envisage a synthesis of Bultmann and Bonhoeffer, and we have already noted that Gregor Smith has had difficulty in relating these two.[2]

However, we ought not to criticize *Honest to God* for failing to do something that may not be possible at all and that, in any case, would demand a much more extended and detailed treatment than was feasible in a small book. Robinson himself speaks in his preface of the intentionally "tentative and exploratory" character of his book, and if we remember this, we may readily concede its merit, not only as a catalyst but also as showing how important trends in recent theology all point to the necessity of raising anew in a radical way the question of God. *Honest to God* was certainly a much better book than most of the things that Robinson has written since, such as *The New Reformation?* Here his eclecticism has run riot. All kinds of different people are quoted and pressed into service, and the result is a very incoherent piece of work that makes it harder than ever to know where the Bishop really stands. If *Honest to God* was also a conflation, it was nevertheless easier to see the main lines and the questions that were raised.

The chief of Bishop Robinson's sources at the time when *Honest to God* was written was Paul Tillich, and Robinson might have done better to stay with Tillich and try to develop his ideas further, for Tillich's whole career was spent in bridging the gulf between Christian faith and secular culture, and it seems to me that he did this with a sanity and balance that have not been surpassed by anyone since. Certainly, he attempted the task at a much more fundamental level than such writers as Robinson, Cox, and van Buren. He was a thinker of considerable stature, and I believe that for a long time to come theologians will continue to find help with their problems through a study of his works. It is true that some younger theologians have expressed impatience with Tillich, and tend to regard him as a speculative theologian who represents an older style of thought. But this is surely unjust. Those who think of Tillich as dwelling in a rarefied atmosphere of abstract ideas need to be reminded that he was one of the first scholars forced to leave Germany when Hitler came to power, and that throughout his career his thinking was related closely to the actualities of human existence.

This last claim may be illustrated from Tillich's thought of God, which is one of the main contributions of his philosophical theology. God, he claimed, must be understood as Being itself.[3] In asking that we should understand God as Being rather than as *another* being, Tillich, it seems to me, overcame or at least pointed the way to overcoming some of the most stubborn difficulties in the way of the traditional theism. Of course, the assertion that God is to be understood as Being rather than as *a* being is by no means new, but perhaps it is receiving a new clarification in our time. I myself have found that Heidegger's philosophy is particularly helpful in clarifying the "ontological difference" between Being and the beings; and Bishop Robinson, in turn, was kind enough to say that my own exposition of God as "gracious Being," based on concepts taken from Heidegger, had clarified his own position.[4] I mention this because it shows us the relevance and importance of Tillich's idea of God. The Bishop had a sound instinct in looking to Tillich for a viable contemporary conception of God, and it is a pity that he has not developed the point further.

But here I must mention that we are still far from having exhausted Tillich's contribution to the understanding of God. If he speaks of God in the language of being, he speaks of him also in the language of "ultimate concern."[5] This expression indicates the existential dimension in Tillich's thought. We can speak or think of God only on the basis of our existential relation to him. Those who criticize Tillich's language about being as abstract and speculative have simply failed to take into account the concept of "ultimate concern" which makes his concept of Being the most concrete as well as the most universal reality. Criticisms based on objections to "metaphysics" are likewise idle. It may well be the case that modern philosophy from Kant onward has discredited the old-style rational metaphysics, but, as Nicolas Berdyaev acutely observed: "It is not true to say that Kant makes an end of all metaphysics; he merely makes an end of metaphysics of the naturalistic rationalist type, metaphysics which are derived from the object, from the world, and he reveals the possibility of metaphysics based on the subject, of a metaphysics of freedom."[6] To avoid confusion, I would prefer to talk here of "ontology" rather than of "metaphysics," and of an "existential ontology" rather than a "metaphysic of the subject." It is clear that with Heidegger and Tillich, we are dealing with such an existential ontology. Moreover, we have already seen that even the secular theologian cannot get by without an ontology.[7] The question is not whether you are going to have an ontology or not, but whether you are going to have an examined ontology or an unexamined one.

Tillich made further valuable contributions to the problem of how to think of God in a secular age, for instance, in his remarks on symbolism. However, we shall leave him for the present, though we shall come back to his ideas in due course.[8]

The second Christian thinker who stood behind Robinson's work in *Honest to God* was Rudolf Bultmann. Even more than Tillich, he took up the questions of religious language and its interpretation, and his theory of demythologizing has been the most valuable contribution to theological hermeneutics in a long time. Bultmann's work was motivated by a number of concerns, and not least among them was a desire to present the Christian faith in a way that the secular mind might be able to understand. The habits of mind of the secularized man are permeated by the ethos of modern science, and this makes the kind of objectified supernaturalism (mythology) of the New Testament unintelligible to him. Thus demythologizing could be described as, at least in part, a secularizing of the language of the New Testament.

However, nearly all critics of Bultmann agree that the idea of God remains very obscure in his thought. Bultmann does not undertake the kind of ontological clarification that we find in Tillich. Of course, he may well have felt that he had no obligation to do this, since he was writing as a New Testament scholar, not as a systematic or philosophical theologian. It is perfectly clear that Bultmann had no wish to consign God to the category of myth. He regards the New Testament message as important only because it is kerygma, the proclamation of an "act" of God. This talk of God's acting remains as an essential element in Bultmann's thought, though one that is not too easily related to his existential interpretation.[9] Apparently afraid of being drawn into illicit metaphysical speculations, Bultmann consistently resists saying anything that might seem to be talk about God as he is "in himself," and maintains that we can talk of God only in terms of his concrete action upon us.[10]

But it seems clear that there is danger here of a complete

subjectivizing of the kerygma. It is not a long step from saying that we can talk of God only as we concretely experience him to the view that "God" is just the mythological name of a certain quality of experience, or of a factor immanent in the human existent.

Helmut Gollwitzer has given a careful analysis of the way in which God might be dissolved away if Bultmann's existential interpretation of the New Testament were carried to extremes.[11] Gollwitzer seems to believe that one of Bultmann's pupils, Herbert Braun, has in fact carried existential interpretation to the point where God, as an independent reality, has been phased out. I do not think, however, that Braun is presenting us with an atheistic version of Christian faith.[12] Insofar as he tries to expound the meaning of the New Testament without using the word "God," this is a perfectly laudable attempt to meet, on his own ground, the secular man for whom God talk has become enigmatic. But Braun surely does not eliminate the reality of God. He finds alternative and—as he hopes —more intelligible ways of talking of this reality. In the end, he makes his equations: "God" is the "whence" of my being stirred up, or, again, the "I may" and the "I ought" (grace and obligation) .[13] Admittedly, what Braun is trying to say is not too clear, and there are passages where the idea of God seems in danger of becoming merged into the web of interpersonal relations. The subjective and anthropological side of the God-man relationship is stressed to such an extent that it is not quite clear whether God is stirring up man or man is stirring up God—whether, if I may be permitted to say so, the dog wags its tail or the tail wags the dog.

One thing that seems to follow clearly from an examination of Braun's position is the necessity for giving some ontological analysis, beyond a merely existential analysis, even if the ontological analysis is based upon the existential one. It is certain that Braun's remarks do imply an ontology, but, as with Bultmann himself, this is left unclear.

Although Bishop Robinson made no mention of Friedrich Gogarten, this is another German theologian who has been powerfully influential in shaping the problematic of God in the secular age. Gogarten was so close to Bultmann in most of his thinking that this is a suitable place to say something about him. Moreover, although Robinson did not draw on Gogarten, two of the other writers whom we have mentioned, Cox and Gregor Smith, are indebted to his thought. But it might be added that among English-speaking theologians, the one standing closest to Gogarten was Carl Michalson, whose untimely death in an airplane accident has robbed American Protestant theology of an outstanding thinker.

Gogarten's view[14] of Christian faith calls, like Bultmann's, for radical demythologizing and existential interpretation. As Gogarten understands it, the process of demythologizing replaces not only mythology but also the static concepts of traditional metaphysics with historical-existential concepts. Along with the demand for demythologizing and existential interpretation, two other major factors contributed to Gogarten's thought. One was his lifelong interest in Luther and his attachment to the Lutheran stress on justification by faith and liberation from the law. The other was an interest in the process of secularization and its relation to Biblical faith; and we may note that Gogarten understood secularization precisely as historicization of human existence (*Vergeschichtlichung der menschlichen Existenz*), that is to say, very much as we have already seen Gregor Smith interpret secularization.

The Pauline notions of inheritance and sonship furnish a powerful inspiration to Gogarten. Once we were children, "under guardians and trustees," but now we "receive adoption as sons." As responsible sons who have now come of age, we have, so to speak, been given the key of the house. We are delivered from tutelage, and stand now in an adult relationship to the Father. This means that we have received the world for our use, and are no longer enslaved to its "elemental spirits" (cf. Gal. 4:1–7).

This teaching does have its relevance in an age when human power and knowledge are expanding so spectacularly. It suggests that this expansion of human power is so far from being a kind of *hybris* that it is rather a responsible stewardship for which man has been destined by God. It is worth noting that Gogarten's thought has impressed one of the greatest Christian physicists of our time—Carl F. von Weizsäcker.[15] But one would have to ask some questions. Is God still of importance, or has he pretty well bowed himself out of the picture? How does this view differ from that of the old-time deists, who believed that God had indeed started things off in the beginning but now takes no further interest in them? These questions would certainly need clear answers if we are to take seriously the notions of stewardship and responsibility in man's dealings with the world.

This talk of the vanishing God leads us to consider the third of Bishop Robinson's sources in *Honest to God*, Dietrich Bonhoeffer. Almost a generation after his death at the hands of the Nazis, he is exercising an extraordinary influence on theology. I find that he has a special fascination for students. No doubt this is partly to be attributed to his heroism and martyrdom. Here was a man who really lived out his faith. It is interesting to note that Ved Mehta put to Eberhard Bethge the question: What is more important—Bonhoeffer's life or his theology? Bethge replied: "Ah, that is a very interesting point. I think the two were closely connected, but I, since I am not an academic type of theologian, would say his life."[16]

The unfortunate thing is that what has caught the imagination has been Bonhoeffer's latest and most fragmentary utterances. Even these have been reduced to slogans—"religionless Christianity," "holy worldliness," "man come of age," and the like. The truth is that very little can be built on Bonhoeffer's last letters, taken by themselves. As Schubert Ogden says: "Bonhoeffer's proposals in these letters are at best hints and suggestions which he was never given the opportunity to work out. The fact remains that what he offers in the way of a constructive statement about God is so insufficiently developed conceptually that it presents no clear alternative to the traditional theism it is intended to supplant."[17]

But the trouble is that Bonhoeffer's views are not treated as the tentative and obscure gropings that they were meant to be. They are invoked, together with the glamour of their author's martyrdom, for confident assertions that may have been very far from Bonhoeffer's mind. My colleague Paul Lehmann, who was a friend of Bonhoeffer in prewar days and who has perhaps as firm a grasp of his thought as anyone, has been constrained to write: "Seldom has an author, living or dead, been so misrepresented by his commentators and translators. . . . The so-called 'death of God' theologians are perhaps the most conspicuous of Bonhoeffer's misrepresenters. They have seized upon the *Letters and Papers from Prison* with such avid and hasty enthusiasm as to have provided an American parallel to those German enthusiasts who have all but launched a 'Bonhoeffer school.' On the continent, 'the world come of age,' 'religionless Christianity,' 'true worldliness' have tempted Bonhoeffer's former pupils, now in theological faculties or church administration, towards cultic passions. In the United States, these same phrases have been appropriated as a kind of quintessential 'new essence of Christianity' which claims Bonhoeffer for the tradition of Nietzsche and celebrates him as the forerunner of a theology without God."[18]

But the fact that Bonhoeffer gets misrepresented cannot be cited as a reason for not paying attention to him. There is no question about his influence in contemporary Protestant theology. We must, however, try to understand his last enigmatic fragments in the light of his whole theological work and as a stage which he reached in the development of that work. More than this, we must pay proper attention to the dialectical elements in these final fragments themselves. They are by no means to be understood only through the more sensational passages. As I shall try to show in later discussions, Bonhoeffer leads us neither to the abandonment of God nor even to the abandonment of "religion," in any reasonable sense of this much-abused word.

Mention of religion brings us finally to say something about the place of Karl Barth as a formative influence in the background of the current debates. There is indeed no direct appeal to Barth in *Honest to God,* as there is to the three other theologians who inspired Robinson's thought. We might even think that Barth, as representative of the so-called "neo-orthodoxy," could not be counted along with the three others. Yet we must remember that

Bonhoeffer drew much of his inspiration from Barth, and although he finally came to criticize Barth along with most other theologians, he bears to the end the Barthian imprint.

Most of the secularizing theologians in Britain and America are ex-Barthians. To some extent, we can think of their present stance as a rebellion against, and then an overcompensation for, the Barthian exaggeration of God's transcendence and the corresponding depreciation of man's "natural" achievements. But there is more to the relationship than this. Already in Barth there are tendencies that, when pushed in a certain direction, can easily lead into a secularized and even atheistic form of theology. Let me mention three elements in Barth's thought that, in varying degrees, have come to new expression among the secularizing theologians: his Christocentrism, his rejection of natural theology, and his critique of religion.

Barth's Christocentrism, which is, of course, found also in Bonhoeffer, has become among the so-called "death of God" theologians an exclusive preoccupation with Jesus of Nazareth. Even some of the orthodox Barthians were occasionally accused of a kind of unitarianism of the second Person, but with writers like van Buren, Hamilton, and Altizer, a further step has been taken. God has faded out, and we are left with the human Jesus as a surrogate for God.

The rejection of natural theology by Barth was counterbalanced by his firm belief in a special revelation. Nevertheless, his attitude was bound to conduce to a philosophical positivism. If, as has happened not only with van Buren but with some philosophical writers, such as Alasdair MacIntyre, one comes to doubt the veracity of the alleged special revelation, then there is nothing left but atheism, either with or without Jesus.

Barth's criticism of religion is simply a consequence of his Christocentrism. If God has made himself known *exclusively* in Jesus Christ and the Biblical tradition, then there can be no truth in the non-Christian religions, and "religion" must be defined, however tendentious or arbitrary the definition may appear to be, as man's attempt to grasp God. This in turn is interpreted along the lines of Feuerbach to mean that the "religious" conceptions of God are simply idols projected by our own minds. Of course, Barth makes an exception for God, the Father of Jesus Christ. This God is not the product of religion, for he has revealed himself. He is the God of revelation, not of religion. But the time would surely come when people would ask: "Well, why make this exception?"

Barth's motive throughout was no doubt to honor Christ, and he was right to uphold the notions of revelation and of God's initiative in granting the knowledge of himself. But Barth narrowed the sphere of revelation too arbitrarily. It is surely outrageous to say, as Barth did in his Gifford Lectures, that "the God of Mohammed is an idol like all other idols."[19] It seems to me impossible to claim that the God of Jesus Christ is *toto caelo* different from God as he is known in Islam, Hinduism, and the rest, and that in the case of the one we must talk of "faith" or "revelation," and in the case of the other of "religion." Of course, Barth recognized that Christianity too becomes a religion and falls under judgment. But he did not call for "religionless" Christianity, acknowledging rather that this religion can be redeemed. However, Barth left himself open to a lot of misunderstanding, and perhaps his followers can hardly be blamed if they have been less subtly dialectical and have fallen into distortions and extravagances. But we shall come back to these problems in due course.

In the meantime, we have perhaps filled in enough of the background to the current debates about God and secularity. We could easily trace the roots farther back— to the social gospel, the Ritschlian movement, and the whole complicated matrix of nineteenth-century thought. But it is unnecessary to do this. Already we have before us so many confused and conflicting tendencies that it will be hard to keep track of them all.

CHAPTER III

The Secular Outlook

Now that we have filled in something of the theological background of the contemporary problem of God, it is time for us to go back to the other pole of our discussion and examine in more detail what we mean by the "secular." We have already had some glimpses of the meanings that have gathered round this word, and in glancing at some of the recent books on the subject, we have found it associated with positivism, with historicality,[1] with the way of life found in a technological and urbanized culture. We have also taken note of the distinction made by some theologians between "secularity" and "secularism."[2] But even so, we are still far from any clear idea of the matter.

Perhaps we can best come to grips with the meaning of the "secular" if we look first of all at the extreme form of the secular outlook on life, that is to say, the form called "secularism." Can we say what this is?

Secularism is not definite enough to be recognized as a specific philosophy. There are many philosophies that could be said to represent a secular point of view, such as materialism, positivism, some kinds of existentialism, and some kinds of empiricism. Secularism is not another type of philosophy to be set alongside these, but, rather, an attitude, a mood, a point of view, a way of noticing and (equally) of failing to notice, that can find expression in many philosophies. It finds expression too in policies of action, where it may be only implicit and has not been raised to the level of conceptual awareness. In such cases, we might call it a "hidden ontology," for such an ontology is grounded not only in thought but also in decision.[3] Secularism, then, is a way of looking on the world and on man's life, and it appears in many different areas of thought and action.

Because of its indefiniteness, no simple definition or description of secularism can be offered. But what can be done usefully is to list a description of some of those areas of life or reality which we commonly call "secular." We would then understand the secularist as the person who is preoccupied with these areas, and whose outlook is more or less exclusively determined by them. In order to sharpen this description of secularism, we shall set over against it at each stage a corresponding description of what the secularist is rejecting; and just as we are depicting secularism in an extreme form, so the kind of Christian faith that we shall set over against it, as rejected by the secularist, will be an extreme form of religiosity or pietism. Both sides may look like caricatures, though, regrettably, both are to be found. This procedure, as well as helping us to clarify some of the essential characteristics of the secular, may also help us to see that any sane resolution of the tension between God and secularity will not embrace either of the extremes undialectically. We shall find ourselves torn between them. This is surely the situation of many people in our time—the very situation that is driving contemporary theology in search of the synthesis between God and secularity.

1. The first thing to be said about the secular is that it is the temporal, as opposed to the eternal. This reflects the original meaning of the Latin word *saeculum*. It means "generation" or "age." Perhaps we could even say that it means "history," human affairs in time. So the secular is that which belongs to this life, to the here and now, to what is going on in this world. When we say "this life," we think of it as opposed to what the Nicene Creed calls "the life of the world to come." We could also say that the secular is the this-worldly, as opposed to what is called the "otherworldly."

The secularist, then, is the man who affirms the temporal, this-worldly character of existence. For him, indeed, an expression like "otherworldly" could only be meaningless unless, perhaps, it stands for an illusory point of view. There is, for the secularist, only this world; there is no other world. The serious-minded secularist, moreover, is concerned with the tasks and the problems of this world. These are surely vast enough to absorb our attention— problems of peace, of justice, of food production, of population control, of education, and of a thousand other matters that cry out for our efforts if the conditions of human life are to be bettered.

What is the opposite position, the one that the secularist rejects? As the secularist sees it, the Christian (or the religious man in general) is more interested in eternity and the otherworldly. (Certainly, he would have only to glance through any of the hymnbooks in common use to have this suspicion confirmed.) Because the mind of the Christian is taken up with the world to come and with the desire to attain to salvation in that world, he is said to neglect the problems of this world and even to sit light to his responsibilities in it.

2. In a more general way, the "secular" is the opposite of the "religious." Man's secular life is taken up by his everyday activities, and of course these occupy by far the greater part of everyone's time: working, producing, eating, sleeping, buying and selling, dealing with one's neighbors, engaging in politics, sport, art, or whatever it may be. To use a common expression, this is "where the action is." Over against these activities are the "religious" practices of those who still care for them: praying, worshiping, singing hymns, fasting, meditating, going on retreats. Do such practices seem shadowy and unreal by comparison with our secular activities?

The secularist certainly thinks so. For him, it is the first group of activities that constitutes the fullness of life. We need not suppose, either, that to confine one's life to the secular sphere means in the slightest degree that one is a sensualist or a pleasure-seeker or a dollar worshiper. I specifically mentioned art and politics among secular activities to show that the secularist can find expression for the desire for beauty or for aspirations after social justice without leaving the sphere of the secular.

Such a secularist is critical of the time that the Christian spends in prayer and worship. He might indeed be tolerant enough to think that these Christian activities are a harmless hobby, and, in any case, he would probably say that he does not understand such things. He might well add that he suspects that prayer and worship are something of an escape for the Christian. They take him away from the real concerns of life into a world of make-believe and inaction. They may, indeed, yield some kind of comforting illusion to those who practice them, but the price paid for this illusion is that the believer is prevented from entering fully into either the enjoyment or the pathos of a truly human existence. I have heard it said, for instance, that neither a Christian nor a Jew can properly appreciate tragedy; this assertion demands some thought at least.

3. In the fields of culture and learning, "secular" knowledge is the kind that is gained by human endeavor and that is based on the exercise of man's rational faculties and his powers of observation. Above all, the natural sciences are taken to exemplify secular learning and to show the effectiveness of an approach that relies on empirical down-to-earth methods. The knowledge gained in this way has a reliability that shows itself in the fact that it enables us to predict the course of events in nature. Above all, this kind of knowledge proves itself in its utility. Over against this secular learning stands theology, which claims to base itself on revelation and seems to be unable to give any clear account of its logical procedures. Perhaps along with theology will be set the old-style metaphysics which, although professing to be a rational study, relied on arm-chair speculation rather than on observation of the phenomena.

The thoroughgoing secularist is usually also a positivist. Only the method of the natural sciences can be accepted as a gateway to genuine knowledge. Even subjects such as history, psychology, and sociology will be esteemed to the extent to which they can show that their methods accord with those of the natural sciences. Usually the secularist will not allow that theology can be considered a legitimate study at all, or that there can be anything such as revelation.

The position of theology as a study of doubtful credentials is sometimes acutely apparent in large secular universities where there are schools or departments of theology. These tend to be isolated from the main life of the university. Some scientists at least retain the memory that theology has been obstructive to the progress of the sciences in the past, and they suspect that the study of theology is not only outdated but even harmful. They may also point to the fact that, in some countries today, scientific and technical progress is held up through prejudices having a religious sanction.

4. There is also a distinctly secular way of conceiving of man himself. We all hear about the "secular man." When we try to spell this out, the conception may not be so distinct, but there are some things we can say. The secular man is the autonomous man. If he is a thoroughgoing secularist, human autonomy is taken to be complete. There is no higher Being than man himself, so man must create his own values, set his own standards and goals, and work out his own salvation. There is nothing transcending man's own powers and intelligence, so he cannot look for any support from beyond himself, though, equally, he need not submit himself to any judgment beyond his own or that of his society.

This autonomous view of man is put forward by existentialists such as Sartre and also by humanists of a more conventional kind. Some writers, having regard to the threats to human existence, see something tragic in man's unaided struggle to subdue the world; others are frankly optimistic and they can point to man's amazing toughness. Up until now, he has in fact made his way. In any case, the secularist finds a certain exhilaration in this thought of man's autonomy. There is a challenge in the situation that calls forth energy and effort.

Contrasted with the autonomous life of the secular man is the life of faith. Whether we call this a life of obedience or of dependence or even of partnership and cooperation, it is not a fully autonomous life. The Christian lives in the faith that over against his own finite being there stands the ultimate Being that meets him in grace and judgment. The secularist objects that the Christian has not really grown up. In the secularist's view, faith is simply a childish clinging to the mentality of the nursery and it stands in the way of an autonomous human freedom and responsibility.

I have deliberately presented this sketch of the secular outlook in such a way as to bring out as sharply as I could the contrast between this view and the one that the secularist rejects. At first sight, there would seem to be no way to bridge the gulf between the two sides. Certainly, our analysis has made it clear that if Christianity were to try to go all the way with the thoroughgoing secularist, this would really be the end of the Christian faith, for it would mean accepting that the immanent actualities of this world are all that is real, that prayer and worship are superfluous or even a mistake, that there is neither grace nor revelation nor God, that no ultimate claim is laid upon us so that we must respond to it in faith. We have seen that van Buren's book did come to just about accepting all these points and he carried through a so-called "reduction" of the faith in order to accommodate them, but such a reduction would be better called an "abolition." The other writers we have talked about would not have conceded every point made by the secularist—and this is why some theologians would rather talk of "secularity" than of "secularism." Thus, to recall two writers whom we have mentioned, Gregor Smith accepts with the secularist the thoroughly historical and temporal character of existence but he rejects positivism and the denial of any transcendence. While Bultmann goes along with the secularist in recognizing the claims of the scientific mentality of our time and in rejecting mythological ideas of the supernatural, he also insists on the radical obedience of man before God and even seems to think of autonomy (*Eigenständigkeit*) as the cardinal human sin.

Although we cannot yield to every demand of the secularist (as outlined in the preceding paragraphs) and remain Christian, I think many Christians would be equally unhappy if they were supposed to accept those positions which the secularist rejects. We have seen that what the secularist complains about are such matters as being so preoccupied with salvation in a world to come that the demands of everyday life are overlooked; with being so immersed in religious practices that the tasks which lie nearer to hand are neglected; with entertaining obscurantist ideas about revelation and the supernatural, and so taking up an antiscientific stance; with depending on God to see things through, rather than putting forth one's own best efforts. Many people would say that this is a mere caricature of Christianity as they understand it, and that if the choice really lay between a thoroughgoing secularism and this kind of unreal piety, they would opt for secularism. I think they would be right and I think we shall find that the true Christian position is not the extreme religiosity that we have seen described, just as we may also discover that true secularity is something different from the rather dogmatic kind of secularism at which we have looked.

Yet we have to say that the secularist's caricature of Christianity has been made possible only because Christians, at one time or another, have projected this kind of image. It is perfectly true, as a matter of historical fact, that Christians—even great Christians—have, in varying degrees, been excessively preoccupied with personal salvation and insensitive to what was going on around them; that they have used religion as an escape; that they have, in the name of the Bible, impeded the progress of the sciences; that they have entertained immature and unworthy ideas of God.

If all this is the case—and how could it be denied?—then the atheism of Marx, Feuerbach, Freud, Nietzsche and others, and the outbursts of some of the "angry young men" in the church, have to be given a hearing, and cannot be dismissed out of hand. Hans Urs von Balthasar has truly written: "The frightening phenomenon of modern atheism may, among other things, be a forcible measure of providence to bring back mankind, and especially Christendom, to a more adequate idea of God."[4] The secularist position has its own excesses and distortions, but these may well have been called forth by excesses and distortions into which Christianity itself had fallen.

What I want to assert, however, is that the sharp dichotomy between "secular" and "religious" on which so much of the current discussion turns is a false dichotomy. When the two extreme positions are set before us, we feel that we cannot subscribe to either and we recognize that both sides, though distortedly, have claims upon us. The genuinely religious man (and I think this would be true of the Jew, the Muslim, and the Buddhist, as well as of the Christian) is by no means unconcerned about the secular, but he refuses to make this the be-all and end-all of his existence if this means denying any transcendent reality, any experiences of grace and revelation. The Christian (or the adherent of one of the other faiths or religions mentioned) does not need to make a choice when faced with the disjunction between a thoroughgoing secularism on the one hand and a false religiosity on the other. He is bound, indeed, to reject both of these erroneous extremes and to choose the more difficult and dialectical path of caring for the secular in the light of faith.

But unfortunately the history of theology (and especially of Protestant theology) has too often consisted of violent swings from one extreme to another. The last generation stressed the transcendent, eschatological character of Christian faith. The rebels who have come on the scene are now insisting on the this-worldly character of Christianity—and it is not surprising that some of the most prominent among them are disillusioned Barthians. They are right in rejecting what Reinhold Niebuhr once called the "transcendental irresponsibility" of neo-orthodoxy but they are wrong in thinking that they must fly to the opposite extreme of a thoroughgoing immanentism.

An example of this exaggerated rush to embrace the secular is provided by the doctrine, taught by several contemporary theologians, that the secular outlook has its foundations in the Bible itself, or even that secularity is the "true meaning" of the Christian gospel. We have already seen a hint of this view in Gogarten,[5] and it may be conceded without hesitation that there is a measure of truth in it. But in some writers, the idea has become wildly exaggerated. They fail to recognize that secularization is too complex a phenomenon to be simply explained in terms of Biblical influences; that the legacy of Greece has been more important in developing the secular mentality than the Bible; that Christianity has, in fact, resisted secularization as far as possible; and, finally, that Christianity could do little else than resist, for a thoroughgoing secularism is quite incompatible with Biblical faith.

Let me illustrate these points by referring to some arguments put forward by Harvey Cox.[6] He tries to show that secularity has been the message of the Bible and the church from the beginning, though it would seem that up until now neither Christians nor secularists have noticed this.

He claims first that the doctrine of creation led to the "disenchantment" of the world, so that it was opened up for scientific investigation and for man's exploitation. Now, there is undoubtedly some truth in this point, and it has often been made before. To believe that God made the world, pronounced it good, and commanded man to subdue it, is to have put behind forever the oppressive pagan superstitions that have weighed so heavily on human life and have sometimes prevented a right use of the creation. But it is an oversimplification to point to this as the major factor in the origin of Western science and technology and in the rise of the secular outlook. One has only to remember that, despite their doctrine of creation, the Hebrews developed no science at all, and that their level of technical civilization was lower than that of their pagan neighbors, such as the Egyptians and the Philistines; and when we remember this, we are put on our guard against any facile connection between the doctrine of creation and the modern outlook.

That the Bible made its contribution to the rise of the Western secular outlook is true, but we have to see this factor along with others that went into the making of Western culture. In his book *Säkularisation*, Arnold Loen has likewise protested against absolutizing the Biblical factor in the rise of Western science and secularism. He sees the "de-demonizing" of the world as the removal of a hindrance to science and technology but claims that the removal of a hindrance cannot be taken as a positive principle for explaining a development.

It is to the Greeks rather than to the Hebrews that we

must look for the origins of Western science and also of secularity. The Ionian philosophers were no longer telling stories of the creation of the world but were asking for a rational account of the nature of things. A dramatic disenchantment of the world occurred when Anaxagoras declared that the sun is not the god Helios, but "a mass of blazing metal, larger than the Peloponnesus." He was prosecuted for impiety and forced into exile, apparently the first victim of the struggle between religion and science.

But the nascent science of Greece was almost wiped out when Christianity and the Bible came on the scene. For instance, as Canon C. E. Raven has pointed out,[7] Aristotle's accurate observations of animals were forgotten and replaced by the bestiaries of the Middle Ages, fantastic books that dealt not with observable facts but with such edifying quasi-Christian legends as how the pelican feeds its young on its own lifeblood. Only with the Renaissance and with the rediscovery through Arab culture of the classical spirit of inquiry did science get going again; even so, it had to fight a continual battle against theological prejudice, from Galileo to Darwin.

The Biblical doctrine of creation may indeed have delivered men from irrational fears of the "principalities and powers" and from being "slaves to the elemental spirits of the universe." But it is going much too far to see in this any more than one among many factors that made possible the rise of Western science, and that not the most important factor. Still less could a doctrine of creation give rise to the autonomous, subjective will to power that has emerged as the characteristic expansive drive of the West and that finds expression in technological dominance of nature. Rather, the Biblical view sanctions neither the superstitious attitude of animism nor the purely secular attitude that lies at the opposite extreme. A doctrine of creation must, rather, see man as God's responsible steward in the world—the "guardian of Being," in a phrase of Heidegger.[8]

Similar criticisms can be made of Cox's subsequent arguments, which attempt to trace what he calls the "desacralization" of politics and the "deconsecration" of values to the Old Testament. It is certainly true that the Biblical writers liberated men for responsible participation in history by abolishing the notion that they are trapped in some fatalistic cycle of events. But surely the Old Testament does lean toward theocracy as the ideal form of government; surely it teaches that the law and ethical values are based in the command of God; surely it teaches that history is under God's providential control, and that he is at work in shaping it.

Once more, one would have to say that the genuinely secular understanding of these matters originated among the Greeks. Thucydides wrote scientific (secular) history, based on the consideration of human motivation and this-worldly events. The Sophists were the first to secularize the conception of law, holding that law is simply human convention—a view utterly unknown in the Bible. Similarly, the Greek *polis,* with its developing democracy, points toward the modern secular state as nothing in the Bible does.

However, it must be insisted again that the Christian position is neither thoroughgoing secularism nor obscurantist submission to supernatural world powers, but, rather, true freedom in the responsible service of God. This is the position that Cox himself wants to establish, but he obscures it by his one-sided praise of secularity.

The most ambitious attempt to show that Christianity is

the forerunner of the secular outlook is surely that of Arend van Leeuwen.[9] In his view, the unfolding of the Christian message has been inseparably bound up with the rise of Western technology. The decline of an explicit Christianity in the West does not, in van Leeuwen's view, imply the dechristianization of the West. It means, rather, that Christianity is now operating in the shape of a technological culture, which may be said to be its secularized form.

The background of van Leewen's thought is to be sought in Barthian theology, intermingled with anthropology and world history. He starts off with some old-fashioned Biblical theology, moving from the conventional contrast between Greek and Hebrew modes of thought and language into a very extended exercise in allegory and typology. Apparently, he has never read James Barr, or, for that matter, other contemporary Biblical scholars, for his appeal is mainly to the writers of a generation ago. The aim of his Biblical theology is to establish the exclusiveness of the Christian revelation, and to discredit the "religions," understood pejoratively, as in Barth.

Next he carries out an extensive survey of world history, in a manner reminiscent of Spengler or Toynbee, though not on such a large scale. It is not going too far to say that the object of this survey is to demonstrate the progressive character and the superiority of Western culture, due, as van Leeuwen supposes, to the Christian elements in that culture. These have finally issued, as we have noted, in secular technology, and this is spreading inevitably and irreversibly through the entire world.

It would be impossible to offer a criticism of van Leeuwen's wide-ranging but loosely organized argument from history. It will be enough to say that it suffers from the same kind of weakness as Spengler's—indeed, it is less convincing than Spengler's. The point is that history is far too protean and ambivalent for anyone to be able to offer with any confidence a theory that ties things up as neatly as these speculative historians do.

But what is most alarming is van Leeuwen's conclusions. He is specially interested in the problem of Christian missions. As he sees it, there can be no alliance or accommodation between Christianity and the great world religions. Christianity is now bound up with technological culture, and the religions stand in the way of its advance. Of course, quite in the Barthian manner, van Leeuwen takes a negative view of non-Christian faiths. He angrily rejects the suggestion that they too may be recipients of grace and revelation. They are survivals from the past, destined to be swept away before the advance of a technological culture that is a secularized Christianity and is the new bearer of the Christian mission.

In fairness to van Leeuwen, I think it ought to be acknowledged that there might well be actual situations in which the Christian might feel that the right tactical decision for him would be to identify with progressive, though secular, forces in a given society, rather than with obstructive, though religious, forces. This might be true even where the religious group was Christian. But what is frightening is the fact that van Leeuwen would seem to have very little sense of kinship with such groups, and seems to be completely dazzled by the technological ideal and its priority over everything else. I doubt if he would have any sympathy with the view of another contemporary writer on the religions, the Catholic scholar Heinz Robert Schlette, who speaks of the affinity that the Christian feels with all who pray, and of how Christianity both gives and receives in its constructive approaches to other faiths.[10] While I have visualized occasions when the Christian might feel constrained to identify with secular rather than religious elements in a given society, I would be bound to add that such occasions would probably be rare. It is the man who prays and is aware of a transcendent reality who, in the long run, is likely to be most concerned with other men as persons; while the man whose mind is fixed on some impersonal ideal, even if it happens to be an admirable one in itself, is the man who can be most inhuman toward his fellows and can use them as means for the realization of his ideal. There are plenty of examples of this in history, and the more someone is convinced of his own rightness and of the wrongness of others, the more likely he is to fall into fanaticism.

I have to agree with Kenneth Cragg's comment on van Leeuwen's thesis: "We would be either strangely naive or incredibly arrogant if we supposed that a technology of which our hemisphere had been the matrix sufficiently represented the world obligations of Christian faith or fulfilled them in the only feasible contemporary form."[11] Cragg does not hesitate to use the word "mischievous"[12] for van Leeuwen's view, and indeed it seems to me that such a view carries into the area of faith something of that aggressive spirit which has been very much a part of Western civilization and has manifested itself in such terrible forms as racism and imperialism.

In the course of this chapter, the shape of the secular has emerged more clearly. The secular has its legitimate claims and rightly condemns all false religiosity. But we have seen too that the secular has possibilities for exaggeration and distortion that are incompatible with Christian faith. Our next task is to consider whether and how we can find God in the secular.

Chapter IV

God in the World

We have seen that the Christian faith, properly understood, does not permit itself to be identified with either
a thoroughgoing secularism or an escapist religiosity. It
cannot allow the sacred to be swallowed up in the secular,
but equally it cannot allow the secular to be reduced to the
level of the unreal (acosmism) through an exclusive concern for the sacred. We cannot allow our world to be cut
in two, calling one sphere secular and the other sacred.
Somehow the Christian has to find a synthesis of the two.
This may mean that he has to see both the sacred and the
secular extending through everything. Dr. A. M. Ramsey,
Archbishop of Canterbury, has remarked that Christianity
is both worldly and otherworldly, and that these two sides
must be held together "in a costly interrelation."[1] In other
words, we must find God in the world.

This, in turn, will mean a new appreciation of the immanence of God. Yet, if we are to avoid being pushed into
a new distortion (pantheism) we must try to recognize
God's immanence without losing sight of his transcendence, on which the last generation of theologians laid
such stress.

We may take our departure from some ideas of Paul
Tillich. I claimed in an earlier chapter[2] that Tillich's way

of seeking to relate Christian faith in God to secular life and thought had not been surpassed—and certainly not surpassed by those theologians who have set up a sharp opposition between secular and sacred, and invite us to choose the former, as if we were presented with an absolute disjunction.

Tillich rejected both the "autonomy" of the secular man and the "heteronomy" of the man who unintelligently submits himself to some external authority. No human being—not even the human race as a whole—is self-contained, and so it cannot be purely autonomous. But to every human existent belongs freedom and responsibility, so that he cannot submit himself to another being without losing his own authentic being. Tillich saw the Christian position in terms of what he called "theonomy."[3] This is one of Tillich's most difficult concepts, but I think the difficulty is resolved when we remember that God is not another being, but Being itself. If God were another being, then theonomy would be just another kind of heteronomy. But if God is understood as Being itself, within which the human self and all other beings have their being, then theonomy overcomes the opposition of autonomy and heteronomy. For the Christian, I suppose one could say that the theonomous principle is the "law of Christ." This is neither the law of his own mind nor a law externally imposed on him, but the inner law of the body of Christ in which he participates.

Tillich conceived his vocation to be "on the boundary," and this is a very suggestive expression for trying to understand the Christian's relation to the reality of God on the one hand and the reality of the secular on the other. Tillich wrote: "At almost every point, I have had to stand between alternative possibilities of existence, to be completely at home in neither and to take no definitive stand

against either."[4] Perhaps we think of him chiefly as standing on the boundary of theology and culture. At any rate,
the Christian stance seems to be on the border, neither
becoming engulfed in a shallow secularism nor yet retreating into a remote otherworldliness. The life of faith is, in
one sense, just living on this border. The Christian is in
the world, in the midst of material realities and human
affairs, a very being-in-the-world; yet just there, he claims
to know a reality that transcends the world, the reality he
calls God. This boundary of which we speak is not a
boundary between two worlds, but rather, the meeting
point of two dimensions belonging to one world.

The thought of man on the boundary and of the tensions
of the Christian faith is by no means new, even if we
today are experiencing it with a new poignancy. The
Christian's situation was well expressed by John Keble in
one of his great hymns:[5]

> Two worlds are ours: 'tis only sin
>   Forbids us to descry
> The mystic heaven and earth within,
>   Plain as the sea and sky.

Two hundred years before Keble, another great Anglican
hymn writer, George Herbert, had expressed a similar
thought in these words:[6]

> A man that looks on glass,
>   On it may stay his eye;
> Or if he pleaseth, through it pass,
>   And then the heaven espy.

Both the hymns from which these stanzas are taken could
be truly described as hymns of the secular. Keble is thinking chiefly of the natural world and Herbert of the routine
chores of everyday life (shortly I shall say more about this
difference); but both men are declaring the worth of these

things and claiming that there is a depth in them that we ought not to miss.

I do not know whether I should say that these two hymn writers are extremely modern or whether I should rather say that some people who think themselves extremely modern are only recovering insights that have always been available in the church. Even the Bishop of Woolwich could hardly find fault with the way in which Keble and Herbert talk about God. They are certainly not talking of a God in some separate realm "up there" or even "out there." They both say quite explicitly that God meets men everywhere, especially in and through the ordinary things, persons, places, and tasks of our everyday existing.

Tillich, as is well known, found the symbol of depth very appropriate for talking of God. God is the depth of experience, that which gives to it a total meaning. Many contemporary theologians have adopted this symbol, for it seems specially apposite for representing the immanence of God and for the conviction that God is to be found in the world rather than beyond it. Surely the symbol of depth is beautifully employed in the two hymns quoted. Keble and Herbert (and likewise Tillich) were too wise to think that depth is the *only* symbol that can speak to man of the holy, and later we shall have to consider more fully the whole question of appropriate ways of thinking about God and the kind of symbols that can be employed.[7] However, in our two hymns, the sacred is understood as the depth of the secular, or, to put it another way, the secular becomes transparent, so that in and through the multiplicity of things and activities belonging to this world we become aware of the one creative Source that holds them all together and maintains them in being. Keble mentions "two worlds," but these two worlds of the sacred and the secular are not worlds apart and are not really separate worlds at all. They are so intertwined that even in the midst of the secular we can give thanks that "Thou, Lord, dost ever create, hallow, fill with life, bless, and bestow upon us all these good things."[8]

We briefly noted that whereas Keble's hymn finds God immanent in nature, Herbert's hymn finds him in the everyday tasks of human work and industry. Because of this, Herbert, though the earlier of the two poets, may have a more direct relevance to our own time.

I might illustrate the difference between the two by recalling two chapels that I visited in the past two years. One was the Chapel of the Transfiguration at the foot of the Rocky Mountains in Wyoming. At the east end, instead of a reredos, there is a plate glass window affording a view of the mountain peaks. Superimposed upon these, as one looks out, is the altar cross. This symbolism does indeed speak of God in the world, present in the majesty of his creation. Yet perhaps to the contemporary person, on vacation from the city, it all seems rather romantic and unreal, and one has the impression that this chapel is more of a tourist attraction than a contemporary place of worship. The other chapel was the Chapel of Industry, part of the new Coventry Cathedral. Here again a clear expanse of window opens out, but the view is of the factories and industrial installations of one of England's most up-to-date cities. This symbolism also speaks of God in the world, but here he is seen in the human efforts and the human relations that twine together in the complex structure of an urban society. Provost Williams writes: "The Chapel of Industry gives the visitor the feeling that the new cathedral is both in and out of the world, a place where the Church gathers its forces before springing out into twentieth-century realities. With its towering walls, the cathedral looks from the outside like a vast medieval stronghold, guarded by St. Michael beside the drawbridge; but its windows give it a kind of vulnerable transparency which is wholly modern."[9]

Nowadays the kind of natural theology that saw God in mountains or stars or clouds has declined. Nature has been made the profane object of scientific research. It may indeed still speak to us obliquely as God's creation, but even so we think of it as an ambiguous witness. If we believe in God, it is not likely to be because in nature we have seen attested his wisdom and beneficence. Rather, if we can still see him in nature, we do so because we already believe in him on other grounds.

When one considers that the world of human affairs is a far richer and more complex reality than a range of mountains, it might be thought that it would be easier to see God in this human world, for if it shows us a wider range of Being, it should be better able to point us to the fullness of Being, which is God. But the human world too is ambiguous, and perhaps seems just as profane and godless as the masses of rock that make up a mountain. Yet if the mountain can point us obliquely to God, so also should the human reality. If God has no place, no presence in the secular world of men in a modern city like Coventry, then it would seem that he has utterly vanished. As Karl Rahner has aptly said, the really important question for the Christian faith today is "whether the Church can so faithfully testify to the redeeming and fulfilling presence of that ineffable mystery whom we call God that the men of the age of technology, who have already made so many advances toward control of their world and destiny, can experience the power of this unspeakable mystery in their lives."[10] We should notice too that nothing less than what Rahner calls "the presence of that ineffable mystery," that is to say, God, would be an adequate experience of Christianity for our time or any time. Certainly, we cannot reduce Christian faith to an ethic and pretend that this is still the apostolic faith or even that it is still something of special importance.

It would seem, then, that it is in the world of men that a contemporary experience of God is to be sought. Yet this would not mean that God's presence in the wider world, that is to say, in his whole creation, is to be set aside, even if we can no longer experience this presence with the directness that men once knew. God is always more than our experience of him, and we cannot contain him in any of our categories, not even the categories of personal relations. It is a weakness of some contemporary theologians, such as Robinson and Braun, that they speak of God so exclusively in terms of the I-Thou encounter that he comes near to being dissolved into a dimension of human existence. This would be a new domestication of God and a new idolatry. His "ineffability" and "mystery" must be guarded by the recognition that although we can say, "Lo, here!" we can never say, "Lo, here and nowhere else."

So it is to the world of men that we turn, to see whether we can find God, or perhaps whether he is trying to find us there. This world of men is the kind of world to be seen from the window of the Chapel of Industry, a "secular" world, as we call it.

When I earlier listed four characteristics of the secular outlook,[11] the first of these was said to be its stress on the temporal and the worldly as opposed to the eternal and the otherworldly. But we have also seen that the Christian, even in the midst of the temporal and the this-worldly, seeks a dimension of transcendence. Does it make sense to do this? In the midst of the social change and the preoccupation with technology, which are characteristic of contemporary cities, can there be any transcendence, or any sense of the unspeakable mystery of God, present, redeeming, and fulfilling?

Let us examine more closely what the Christian's quest for transcendence means. The Christian attitude in the face of the contemporary world may very well be described in a phrase of Alec Vidler's, reflecting in turn the thought of Bonhoeffer—"holy worldliness." This means an acceptance of and an involvement in the world—this material world where God has been pleased to set us. Yet always there must be a searching below the surface of things for the holy depths that give meaning to this whole worldly existence and rescue it from pointlessness, if not indeed from sheer absurdity.

Here it must be said with regret that the trouble with some of our less responsible contemporary Christian secularizers is that they have taken up the ideal of holy worldliness, but seem to have promptly forgotten the adjective and reduced the ideal to a worldly concern *tout court*. They tell us that Christianity is a purely secular movement, their ideal of the good life seems scarcely distinguishable from the one that is so assiduously propagated by Madison Avenue, and the more extreme among them, in their horror at any supposed "withdrawal" from the world, come near to advocating that the time has arrived to replace poverty, chastity, and obedience with affluence, promiscuity, and autonomy as the highest goals for human life, or even as the new evangelical counsels!

The slogan for all this is that we should "say yes" to the world. But I do not think that a simple world affirmation will either help us to find God in the world or help the world to know his presence. God himself says both "yes" and "no." So does Christ and the New Testament, and so must the church if it is to be true both to itself and to the very world toward which it has a mission. A "yes-man" gains no one's respect, and is a weakling.

It is interesting to note that Bonhoeffer, though he advocated a "worldly" Christianity, made it perfectly explicit that the kind of worldliness that he had in mind has nothing to do with the immersion in material pursuits and enjoyments that we commonly associate with the "worldly" man. Bonhoeffer makes a statement that ought to be pondered by those who invoke his support for a thoroughly secularized Christianity. He says: "In Christ we are offered the possibility of partaking in the reality of God and in the reality of the world, *but not in the one without the other*. The reality of God discloses itself only by setting me entirely in the reality of the world, and when I encounter the reality of the world, it is always already sustained, accepted and reconciled in the reality of God."[12] There is a dialectic here that takes us beyond any naïve world affirmation, just as it rules out any false religiosity. God is met in the world, but the world is known in its reality only as God's world.

Of course, the teaching of the New Testament on these matters is plain enough, and exhibits the same kind of dialectic. Christ was undoubtedly concerned for men's bodies and for physical realities. Both by command and example, he made it plain that if his followers would obey God, they must strive to meet the physical needs of their neighbors and promote their material well-being. But when he was tempted to turn stones to bread, that is to say, to proclaim a secular gospel with the satisfaction of economic needs at its center, his answer was definite enough: "Man shall not live by bread alone, but by every word that proceeds from the mouth of God" (Matt. 4:4). You cannot turn a half-truth into a whole gospel.

The tension that characterizes the Christian's relation to the world is brought out very clearly in John's Gospel, where it is a recurring theme. On the one hand, God has loved the world and gone to the utmost lengths for its salvation; on the other hand, the world is represented as hostile to God and to the Christ whom he has sent. The paradox is stated in our Lord's intercessions for his disciples: "I do not pray that thou shouldst take them out of the world. . . . They are not of the world, even as I am not of the world. . . . As thou didst send me into the world, so I have sent them into the world" (John 17:15–18). These words certainly imply a commission to live and serve in the world, and yet, with equal certainty, they imply that the being of the Christian transcends a merely worldly horizon.

Just as God has loved the world, so the church must love the world; and it must serve the world, however costly that service may be. The prayer draws a parallel between the church's mission in the world and that of Jesus. This parallel undoubtedly needs to be preached again and again if the church is not going to fall victim to the ever-present temptation to turn itself into some cozy retreat where the faithful gather round their table and forget about what lies outside their own charmed circle. But if we say that the church must serve the world, we must also say that it would serve the world ill if it merely conformed to the world's ways. To say "yes" to the world does not mean becoming the world's "yes-man," so to speak. The church says "yes" to the world in the context of God's action in the world, an action that transfigures the world.

The church would not serve the world by capitulating to it. Rather, the church's aim must be to awaken the world to a true understanding of itself, and this means an understanding of itself within a fuller reality, so that it does not idolize itself but knows itself as God's creation; or. to put it another way, the church's task is to help man in the world to see beneath the surface of worldly things and everyday relationships to the holy depths that can give meaning and worth. This mission of the church to the world was surely never more urgent than it is today in the technological age, with all its promise of material abundance and secular prosperity, yet with all its threat of superficiality, emptiness, and the devaluation of personal life.

The church serves the world not by capitulating to it but by maintaining a dialectical attitude that both accepts and rejects, and in everything seeks to bring both church and world to deeper self-understanding. The dialectic expresses itself in a whole range of vocations, from those that are most deeply involved in the "secular" activities of the world to the specific ministries of the church; and there is a place within this range of vocations for the men and women who have responded to the call to the "religious" life, and who equally serve the world by witnessing to the realities of prayer and of the life of the spirit.

If the church is to be effective in its mission in the secular age, and if it is to realize for itself and for mankind generally the presence of God in the complex world of today, there will have to be many Christians who, without merely conforming themselves to the world, are willing to take the risk of being in earnest about going into the world and sharing, even with those who reject their faith, the battle to overcome the evils afflicting the world. No doubt there are risks here as well as opportunities, and the history of the worker-priest movement has shown something of both. But if the Christian faith really does bring grace and reconciliation, it need not fear to expose itself to rival faiths in the midst of the world. Perhaps it could even be in the striving and sharing together of the Christian and the "secular" man (could it even be here alone?) that the eyes of the secular man are opened to those wider realities of which the Christian knows; for, as we seek to satisfy human need, we learn more and more of the depth of that need. The moment comes when the merely worldly is seen to be inadequate to an authentic human existence. By the "merely worldly" I mean the things of this world cut off from deeper levels of reality. To come to this point of recognition is to attain the understanding that men, to live as men in the fullest sense, need more than bread and can be fulfilled only in God.

The point has been very well made by Arthur Vogel. The modern technological world is a world of man's making. Therefore he can never find his whole self within that world, for he is not his own product. "Our being inexorably drives us beyond any given state of ourselves or our world."[13]

To know the world in its depth, and to know ourselves in the depth is already to know something of the mysterious transcendence that embraces the world and ourselves and that promises a meaning and wholeness that we could not otherwise find.

Although perhaps his argument employed a style of philosophizing that nowadays has gone out of fashion, there is still much to learn from Alfred Edward Taylor's consideration of the kind of good that man, by his very constitution, is driven to seek.[14] Taylor points out that what is characteristic of our temporal life is its successiveness. It consists of one thing after another, and of necessity every gain is accompanied by a loss, which to some extent cancels it out. For instance, as an individual gains the wisdom of experience, he loses the spontaneity and adventurousness of youth. He may no longer have the will or the energy to carry out the policies that he is at last able to conceive of in a mature way. Something similar could be said about the life of a nation or a society, and this is surely very clear to us in the ambiguities of the contemporary world. As Taylor says: "However much we gain in the way of good by what we call an advance in civilization, something which is also good has to be surrendered."[15]

Now, perhaps it just is the case that human life is like this. Perhaps the universe just does not make sense, and there is built into all human striving and aspiration the outcome of disappointment and frustration. But surely all human striving for the better, whether individual or social, is motivated by the hope—or, one may say, the faith— that the universe does make sense, that our aspirations and efforts are worthwhile, that there is not only a better but a best. This widespread phenomenon of a deep confidence in life is mentioned several times by Schubert Ogden in *The Reality of God* as evidence of a kind of implicit belief in God. Certainly, as Taylor argues, it points to a tendency deep within man to look beyond (or through, or beneath, according to the symbolism preferred) the secular multiplicity of things and events for a unity that gathers them up. In the very depths of our being, whether we are Christians or secularists or something of both, there lie aspirations that, as they unfold themselves, carry us beyond the merely transient and worldly, and which can rest only in the *summum bonum,* in God himself.

But if the end transcends the world, nevertheless the way to that end lies through the world. To the extent that he is willing to join with all men of goodwill in tackling the problems nearest to hand in the world, the Christian may hope by his work and witness to open for himself and others that deeper dimension of grace that makes all the difference between shallow worldliness and holy worldliness.

CHAPTER V

Religionless Christianity?

An expression that we frequently hear nowadays is "religionless Christianity." It is an imprecise slogan that is very hard to pin down, and it gets used in different ways by different people. William Hamilton makes a useful distinction between the "moderate" religionlessness of people such as Bishop Robinson who want to reduce or change such "religious" activities as liturgy, prayer, and the like, and the more extreme religionlessness of those who see no need for God at all.[1] Obviously there are many degrees of religionlessness. In any case, the phenomenon corresponds to what we identified as the second major characteristic in our analysis of the secular outlook.[2] It will be remembered that the secularist called for the devotion of human energies to concrete, everyday tasks rather than to such airy ongoings as prayer. Religionless Christianity is part of the secularizing process within the Christian faith, and like other aspects of that process, it contains real insights mixed with extravagances. As far as the question of God is concerned, the tendency toward "religionlessness" tends to play down the sense of dependence on God and to lay stress on human activity, especially activity in the ethical sphere. In its mildest form, religionless Christianity may amount to no more than some tinkering with the liturgy. In its extreme form, it means the abolition of all prayer and worship and the transformation of Christianity from a religious faith into a humanistic ethic of love, centered on Jesus.

The question about religionless Christianity is not only one of how far the religionlessness goes; it is complicated further by the notorious multiplicity of meanings that have been attached to the word "religion." There must be hundreds of definitions of "religion," some more and some less adequate, and many of them frankly "loaded," either for or against. We have already mentioned Barth's antipathy to religion, which he considered to be man's attempt to grasp God.[3] Of course, in attacking religion, Barth did not mean to abolish God or prayer, for against religion he set "revelation," and claimed that the true God had made himself known in Christ. However, I would say myself that revelation, grace, and reconciliation are known to non-Christians too, so that if one is going to call Christianity a "faith" rather than a "religion," one ought to be ready to extend the same courtesy to Islam, Hinduism, and the rest.

Barth's attack on religion was largely a matter of arbitrary semantics. You exchanged "religion" for "revelation," but you still trusted in God. The new exponents of religionless Christianity, or some of them, are prepared to call the revelation, too, in question.

This indicates that the disaffection with religion goes beyond any semantic question. It is not that people have turned against "grasping at God" (if they ever were addicted to such an improbable pastime) but are still willing to let him reveal himself. They do not expect him to reveal himself, either. In fact, the distinction between "religion" and "revelation" was badly made by Barth. I suppose we might say that "religion" is the outward form of liturgy and the like that grows around man's response to any revelation. Because man has an embodied, historical existence, religion is, in my opinion, inseparable from revelation. James Barr has recently made the same claim for Biblical religion: "It is a misfortune and disadvantage of a revelational theology that it tends to produce a marked value difference between the concepts of revelation and religion. . . . Revelation not only produces, but depends on religion."[4]

Of course, even those who put a positive valuation on religion would be willing to agree that religion can go bad. Perhaps the more they value religion, the more ready they would be to admit this, because precisely those things which have the highest potential can become the worst when they are perverted. We need hardly be reminded that there has been much religion in the world that has been marked by superstitious beliefs and sometimes by cruel and degrading rites. These corrupt forms of religion have not been confined to pagan cults. Christianity too has had its full share of distortions and has issued in fanaticism, hatred, and persecution, sometimes directed against non-Christians, sometimes against fellow Christians.

The champion of religion will probably tell us that these unhappy features of religion are a falling away from its true insights and that nothing should be judged by what is worst in it. But the secularist might well reply that these perversions have been all too common and that if religion were all that it has been claimed to be, then there would not have been so many ugly episodes in its history. We have already noted that the secularist asks us to throw our energies into the betterment and enjoyment of our everyday life in this world instead of letting them be diverted by religious loyalties. Such loyalties, as he sees them, can be harmful in a number of ways. They can be divisive or wasteful of resources that could be put to better use or an excuse for not coming to grips with the real moral and social issues of our time.

Because they have been impressed by such considerations, some Christians have begun to look for a "religionless" Christianity. As it seems to them, a genuine Christian faith, streamlined to the needs of the modern world, needs to be freed from the cumbersome apparatus of religion.

No doubt there is much truth in what they say. If religion is not to fall into the distortions that continually threaten it, it needs to be under constant scrutiny and criticism, and we may be glad that this criticism is not left to outsiders, but that some of it comes from men and women within the Christian community. Actually, the most valid and searching criticisms must come from insiders, for only those who participate in the Christian community of faith can have a proper understanding of its life; and only those who have such an understanding can know how far short the Christian "religion," with its institutional apparatus, is falling in regard to the revelation and faith response that it is meant to express. By comparison, the criticisms of outsiders are superficial. This does not mean that one need not listen to criticisms from outside, and the church is, in fact, becoming increasingly aware of the need for dialogue not only with other religions but also with humanists, Marxists, and the like.

Yet the most radical critics of religion have always spoken from within, and have been men with a clear and imperative vision of God. Such were the Hebrew prophets, summoning men from empty cults to a relation of genuine obedience before the Lord God. Then, in course of time, no one could have been more forthright than Jesus Christ in his condemnation of the false religiosity of the Pharisees, for only he who knew the supreme importance of a right relation to God could clearly perceive every distortion of that relation. In the early days of the church, controversy over religious practices was already widespread, and we find the apostles deciding that Gentile converts must not be overburdened by ritual or legal regulations carried over from the religion of the Jews.

In each of the cases mentioned, religion had to be criticized in order that the spontaneity of faith might not be smothered. The danger is an ever-present one. Such criticisms of religion are just, and when we hear them from some of the theologians of our own time, we must recognize that these men are continuing the prophetic tradition. If religion is to be saved from the perversion and deterioration that threaten it, it must be steadily subjected to the criticism that is made in the name of faith itself. All too readily religion domesticates and neutralizes whatever might be disturbing and demanding in God's self-revelation; it becomes turned in upon itself rather than outward upon the tasks of mission and service; it comes to overprize its institutions and forms, so that it shrinks from the risks and ventures that are demanded of it; at the very worst, it can become an outward show, a way of winning esteem in the eyes of others, although in our hearts we may care little for it. It is both right and inevitable that some bolder spirits will become angry and impatient with structures that, as they believe, have become too rigid, and there must be a readiness to listen to such voices and to be open to renewal.

But in this matter as in so many others, we have not

only to listen but to listen *critically,* accepting the just strictures of the advocates of religionless Christianity but rejecting what is doctrinaire and shortsighted and refusing to be pushed to extremes that would be just as much distortions as the positions that they are supposed to remedy. The criticism of a religion that has gone bad becomes absurd and even harmful if it develops into an indiscriminate attack on all religion. Unfortunately, something like this does happen among some of the advocates of a so-called "religionless" Christianity.

Let us pass in review some of the commoner criticisms of religion that are currently being made. We shall find that each of them has a measure of validity, but that it does not reach beyond a certain point.

1. The objection is made that religion involves us in a superstitious reliance on a *deus ex machina,* in a false supernaturalism or an outmoded metaphysic. This in turn diminishes human effort and the sense of human responsibility. There is every need to urge this objection against much of what passes for religion, and is in fact childish, looking on God as a useful problem solver or a convenient explanation for anything that might not be easily understood. Surely the effect of the objection is simply that it makes us think harder about God and his relation to the world and man's life. This idea of God has already advanced a long way from primitive conceptions, and what seems to be now required is that the idea should be further developed and made more adult. But this means that so long as we pray and worship and talk about the transcendent (and most advocates of religionless Christianity do all these things) we are not delivered from the basic religious conviction, which, however we express it, most certainly implies some kind of ontology, some kind of belief

about the way things are. We cannot pray or talk of the
transcendent or even of an ultimate commitment without
being prepared to state some kind of rationale for these
things. Indeed, I believe that in a sense it could be said
that every man is, in virtue of being a man, ontological.[5]
Probably even the Christian who professes to reject God
and the transcendent altogether (the so-called "death of
God" theology) has his own ontology; and certainly nothing
short of this extreme position could claim to be "religionless," in any meaningful sense.

2. A further objection to religion is that it has to do
with the individual's quest for salvation, and is thus inherently egocentric. This would certainly apply to Protestant evangelicalism and pietism, in some of its forms, and
to Catholic pseudomysticism as well as to a great deal of
popular Catholic devotion. But the objection completely
misses the main line of Christian piety, centered on the
Eucharist. The whole sacramental life implies the notion
of incorporation and of the *corpus Christi*. And this is not
a collective selfishness, for the body of Christ is understood
as the firstfruits of creation, or as the leaven spread through
the whole and working in the whole. The objection simply
declares that the quest for salvation or wholeness must
have in view nothing less than all mankind; while this
condemns some distortions of religion, it reaffirms the purpose that lies at the heart of all true religion.

3. Religion easily becomes idolatry—a fetishism in
which things meant to serve the cult become the objects
of the cult. People become fanatically attached to particular dogmatic formulations or particular institutions. Rules
are made absolute and immutable. Even the Bible can
become a fetish, as it has among fundamentalists. The
process whereby fetishes and idols are set up needs to be

constantly combated with every weapon of criticism and satire. Religion itself carries out this kind of reformation, and it would seem that only reformation *from within* is effective. When that which has been made a fetish is deprived of its demonic, usurped power, it is not abolished but restored to its right use in the service of the community of faith. No faith can survive—and certainly not as the faith of a community—without some outward forms. Almost inevitably, these eventually acquire a life of their own and threaten to smother faith itself. But every community seems to have a power of renewal, and from time to time does, in fact, reform and renew itself. This is true not only of the Christian church but of other communities of faith as well. There is a story of a Buddhist master who arrived at a shrine in the middle of very cold weather. He took down one of the images of the Buddha and made a fire of it.[6] This is a good illustration of what might be called "religionless Buddhism." It makes excellent sense in context, and values the spirit above the letter; but it is no warrant for a general iconoclasm—this, indeed, would be a new fanatacism. It is interesting to note that Gabriel Vahanian, one of the initiators of the recent controversies over the "death of God" and perhaps the theological writer who has most horror of idolatry, has accused his fellow proclaimers of the death of God on the ground that they have turned this into a new fetish! But perhaps the simple truth is that man, as an embodied creature in the world, needs some institutions, some symbols, some rites around which to organize his beliefs. Even iconoclasts have something of the sort, and if one considers the history of Puritan sects, they have by no means been free from idolatries.

4. Still another criticism of religion is that it tends to be a separate department of life, and hence a distraction, an

escape, or a luxury. This too must be conceded, and the preceding chapter was devoted precisely to the question of how faith can operate out in the world. Ideally, there should be no separate church buildings, no special day of worship, no times set aside for prayer, no specifically religious activities, for the spirit and meaning of faith should pervade everything that is done and find its full expression there. This is indeed how it will be in the consummation, or so the Christian may believe. But it would be utopian to suppose that we are anywhere near to there at the present. Who would be optimistic enough to suggest that the Christian spirit has so thoroughly permeated the life of the world that the specific community of faith can now be disbanded and its activities discontinued? Nevertheless, this fourth objection to religion is a constant reminder that the Christian community must be a porous one, with roughly defined edges that allow it to merge with the world. God's saving work, we believe, is directed to the whole world, not just to the elect, as some have supposed; or, better expressed, all are elect, not just some favored elite.

The objections to religion, then, have their undoubted validity, but this extends only up to a point, and the advocates of religionless Christianity often want to go beyond this point, though, as we have seen, they are divided among themselves about how much religion they want to abolish and how much they want to keep. The trouble with many of these people is not that they are too sophisticated or too *avant-garde,* but that they are not sophisticated enough. They oversimplify the problem by setting up a false disjunction between ethics and religion, and suggest that the Christian is faced with a choice between getting involved in action in the world or else retreating into an unreal atmosphere of ineffective piety. This is quite an untrue picture of the situation. I would suggest that, on the contrary, there can be no sustained intelligent Christian action that is not informed and supported by prayer and meditation on the meaning of Christian faith, just as Christ's own deeds of love were intimately associated with his communing with the Father. On the other hand, it has also to be affirmed that there is no genuine prayer or worship that does not, so to speak, spill over from the sanctuary into the affairs of daily life.

It seems to me that there are two decisive questions that have to be addressed to the advocates of religionless Christianity. The first is whether they still attach any importance to the Christian ideas of sin and grace. Admittedly, these are difficult to conceptualize in a satisfying way, but the realities to which the words "sin" and "grace" point have always been well known in Christian experience. It has been believed that the Christian ethic, and especially Christian love, is made possible through an act of God that delivers man from the self-centeredness of sin and renews him through grace; it has likewise been believed that if the Christian is to continue in a "state of grace" (which is not a permanent "state" at all), this can happen only through such prayer and communion with God in Christ as will shape his decisions. Are we now being told that the Christian ethic does not need this "religious" support? The second question to be asked is whether Christian life and character need a process of training, discipline, and formation before proficiency in them can be attained. This question is independent of the first and can be asked no matter how the first gets answered. It is the question really of whether the Christian life is an easy matter, or whether (for most people, at least) it is a very difficult demand. Frederick Herzog has put the matter well when he writes: "Christian decision-making today is often represented as altogether too easy a matter. In some cases it would seem as though nothing else were required as a basis for action than a general grasp of human love." But he goes on: "We cannot expect that costly love will be an easy reflex. It must be learned."[7] How is it going to be learned except through the kind of exercises and discipline that are customarily called "religious"? Certainly it will never be learned from a few sentimental platitudes about the "man for others."

Let me illustrate these points from a brief consideration of Dietrich Bonhoeffer. He is usually regarded as a leading apostle of "religionless" Christianity, but whatever he may have meant by that, I think he was undoubtedly a champion of the kind of religion I am defending in this chapter —the religion of grace, and the religion of prayer and worship.

Probably Bonhoeffer's most important book was his *Ethics,* though he did not live to put it in final shape. In this book he teaches that the Christian, even if he is ultimately concerned with the "last things," must be immediately concerned with the things that are "next to last," that is to say, with the things of this world. It is amid these that we find ourselves, and it is through them that our path lies. We considered this in the preceding chapter, and acknowledged the value of a "holy worldliness."

But how did Bonhoeffer conceive of the possibility of a Christian ethic in the midst of these "next to last" things? It seems to me that the key word in his ethics is "conformation." The Christian is a man who is being conformed to Christ. This takes place when, to quote Bonhoeffer's own words, "the form of Jesus Christ works upon us in such a manner that it molds our form in its own likeness."[8] But how can this happen? Bonhoeffer is quite clear that it does not happen because of our own efforts of will "to be like Jesus." It is a work of grace, something that happens to us. When it does happen in men, surely it happens because they have, as it were, let Christ penetrate into their being; because through prayer, meditation, worship, the sacraments (in a word, religion), their lives have been touched and transformed by the same God who was in Christ. If this is religion, then religion is fundamental to the Christian ethic.

These remarks find their confirmation when we look at Bonhoeffer's *Letters and Papers from Prison,* and see how he spent his last months in a Nazi jail. Perhaps the first thing to do is to try to put these letters into their historical context. Bonhoeffer was indeed in a religionless environment, where Christianity had been flatly rejected. We may recall that Hans Kerrl, the Nazi minister for cultural affairs, had bluntly declared that the Germany of the future would be a state without a church.[9] Perhaps Bonhoeffer recognized that in an increasingly secularized world a time might come when Christianity everywhere would be deprived of the recognition and privileges that it had once enjoyed. In any case, he did conclude that Christians would have to depend more and more on the inward resources of faith, and less and less on outward supports. To this extent, they would have to become more adult in their faith, in the face of a world that it has become customary to call "post-Christian." But if Christians have to live without some of the outward supports and reminders that were available in the more "religious" epochs in history, this does not mean in the slightest that they have to live without those spiritual practices which constitute the real core of religion. Bonhoeffer tells us that in prison he found strength—the strength that he needed for his eventual martyrdom—in daily prayer, and in reading the psalms and Scriptures in course.

As Martin Thornton has pointed out in a book that makes a unique and important contribution to the present theological debates, Bonhoeffer was, in fact, attesting to the value of something very like the daily offices.[10] Thornton's whole treatment of religionless Christianity is most instructive, since it comes from one who has a true appreciation for both modern thought and traditional spirituality. He sees a parallel between the adult kind of faith of which Bonhoeffer wrote and the state of "habitual recollection" attained by persons who have progressed far in the spiritual life. Just as Bonhoeffer recognized a kind of faith that could be sustained in the absence of some of the outward supports that were common in earlier times, so the person who has reached the maturity of habitual recollection enjoys a steady awareness of God's presence and no longer needs too many outward reminders. He is already, as it were, living in a manner that is fully eschatological.

But just because of his deep and sympathetic understanding of these matters, Thornton is able to show in the most devastating way the weakness and indeed the folly of the extreme advocates of a religionless Christianity. They have failed to understand that the condition of spiritual maturity is not something that can be attained overnight, but only through discipline and training. The way to this maturity lies through prayer, worship, and devotion, and, one may add, through perseverance in these things even in times of aridity, when it all seems rather futile.

Certainly, our prayers and worship are all in vain if they make no difference to our lives or to the way we treat our neighbors; we have already conceded that we always need critics of religion to remind us of this. But some of the contemporary critics are extraordinarily shallow and naïve. Their "religionless" Christianity turns out to be an "instant" Christianity, and this is merely silly.

It seems to me that in the last resort our objection to religionless Christianity is that it brings us perilously near to a subtle kind of spiritual pride. It obscures the fact that we are embodied creatures, not angels, so that we need a discipline to shape our lives and bring them to maturity. It wants to hurry to the end, without traversing what may well be a rough and painful road leading there.

Furthermore, the adherents of the idea of religionlessness tend to overlook the moral weakness of ordinary, sinful human beings. They sometimes tell us contemptuously that religion is a crutch. But those who are aware of sin in human life are thankful to have a crutch. They hope that as they go along they may reach a stage when the crutch will not be needed anymore. But perhaps that will only be when they come to the immediate presence of God, when God is all and in all, for then work and worship and all life will be one and undistinguishable. But that *eschaton* is reached by few in their everyday life here. Most of us move only slowly and with difficulty. Certainly, neither here nor even in the *eschaton* can we live the full life into which we are called, without the divine grace. And how do we now receive that grace, except through joining in the prayers, sacraments, and devotions of the worshiping community—in religion?

This is not a withdrawal from life or a luxury or some rival claimant for our energies. It is, rather, our bond with God, conforming the Christian to Christ. This kind of religion needs no excuse.

CHAPTER VI

God and Contemporary Thought

The third point that was made in our analysis of the secular outlook[1] concerned the reliability and prestige of so-called "secular" knowledge as contrasted with the doubtful status of theology and of religious knowledge generally. Can the theologian today vindicate the claims of faith, or show that there is a knowledge of God and of man having its own reasonableness, such as entitles it to a place in the spectrum of the thought of intelligent, educated people? Or is there just no way to bridge the gap between the assertions of faith and the convictions of contemporary science and philosophy?

I do not think that it is any answer to this situation to make an appeal to special revelation. That there are revelatory experiences, I do not doubt for a moment, but we also need an apologetic that will mediate between the revelation and the secular thinking of our time. If anyone chooses to call this "natural theology," I have no objection, but what I have in mind is not the old-fashioned natural theology that set out to prove the existence and beneficence of God from some universally accepted premises about the world. Rather, I visualize a theology of interpretation that will try to make sense of the claim to have had a revelatory experience of God and will relate this kind of experience to our everyday experience. In order to do this, our natural theology or apologetic will have to immerse itself in the thought forms of our time.

In rejecting the appeal to special revelation to establish the reality of God, and in setting aside, likewise, the classic natural theology as employing an outmoded conceptuality and a dubious metaphysical method, I am simply saying that the gospel must meet men where they are and talk the language that they understand. Surely this task is implied in the gospel itself, for the very substance of its message is that God has come into the midst of human life. It tells how the eternally begotten Son "came down from heaven, and was incarnate by the Holy Ghost of the Virgin Mary, and was made man."

God does not dwell apart, but takes the risk of meeting men in the midst of the world. This good news about God must also be incarnated in the world's language. If the church is to teach and preach the gospel of a God of love, its message must be brought out from the dimly understood and half-forgotten language and concepts of former times into the language and concepts that are current today.

Of course, there is a risk in this. The risk is that the essential truths of the Christian faith may be lost in the process. They may be absorbed into the new mentality in such a way that they get diluted or distorted as we try to make them relevant to our contemporary world. Unfortunately, theologians and preachers often do fall into this kind of error, and we have the pathetic spectacle of well-meaning men who are so anxious to obtain a hearing for Christianity that they turn it into something so harmless and universally acceptable that it has also been made empty and without power. It becomes just an appendage of the culture, conformed to the world in every way so that it may give no offense. We must always be on our guard against this.

But just as God presumably took a risk in the incarnation, so the church has to take a risk if it is not going to let the gospel be shut up within the little ecclesiastical world, but believes that this gospel is something to be proclaimed to men. The risk has in fact been taken again and again by the church throughout its history. It was taken by Paul at Athens when he spoke of the cult of an unknown God and when he cited the verses of a pagan poet, and found in those things belonging to the religion of the people, points of contact through which he could introduce the message of Jesus Christ. The same risk was taken by the great Christian doctors of the early centuries as they drew on the resources of Greek philosophy for the articulation and communication of Christian truth.

One of the most instructive examples of an apologist in the history of the church is Thomas Aquinas. The editor of the new edition of the *Summa Theologiae,* Thomas Gilbey, O.P., has written: "St. Thomas' leaving Monte Cassino and becoming a man of Paris exemplified the emergence of the great questions of human debate into what was changing into a secular world."[2] It is interesting to notice that this quotation envisages the process of secularization as already going on in the thirteenth century.

But in any case, Thomas Aquinas took the risk of getting into the secular cultural environment of his time, and of talking its language. Nowadays we think of him almost as the standard of orthodoxy, but many of his contemporaries were very suspicious of what he was doing, and some of his views were actually subjected to episcopal censure. It is surely a strange irony to recall that both the illustrious sees of Paris and Canterbury were once extremely negative in their attitude toward Thomas Aquinas' teaching!

Yet Thomas Aquinas must have seemed a very dangerous person to many churchmen back in the thirteenth century. At that time, the philosophy of Aristotle, as transmitted and developed by Arab thinkers, was undergoing a powerful revival in the great universities of Europe. It seemed to some that this philosophy could be accepted as itself a sufficient system of belief on which a serious man could base his life, apart from any appeal to the Christian revelation. In this sense, it was truly a secular philosophy, just as at a later time idealism and existentialism were to offer themselves as philosophies of life complete in themselves apart from any specifically religious foundation.

But Thomas Aquinas in many ways showed himself to be the ideal apologist. He did not waste time in merely negative denunciations of a philosophy that had already captured the imagination of many of the brightest minds. He did not try the impossible task of trying to put the clock back. On the other hand, he did not tamely capitulate to the philosophic mood of his day, as if it must be allowed the last word on everything. What Thomas Aquinas did was to accept everything that he found true and useful in this philosophy and to bring it into fruitful contact with the still greater truths he had learned from the Christian revelation. Also, he did not merely use the philosophy of his time as an apologetic device but deployed its categories in a magnificent articulation and exposition of the Christian faith. He accepted not only the language but much of the rational and empirical spirit of Aristotelianism, and used these to give to Christianity probably the most powerful and persuasive statement it has ever received.

Thomas Aquinas, then, took the risk of going into the world of secular thought and learning. We may be glad that he did, for it turned out to be an eminently justified risk. But he took the risk in obedience to the gospel itself, and this was the fundamental loyalty to which his thought remained subject. This, as much as his mastery of secular thought forms, is what constitutes his greatness as an apologetic theologian, that is to say, a theologian who addresses the world that lies outside the doors of the church.

If the gospel is to be heard in the modern world, where secularization has been carried far beyond what Thomas Aquinas knew, then again there will have to be taken the intellectual risk of thinking in the thought forms of this world, though once more the taking of the risk must be coupled with an obedience to the gospel. But is it possible to think the Christian truths in the thought forms of today? Perhaps it will sometimes seem that there is so little in the secularized thought of today that is hospitable to Christian truth, and so much that seems just plain hostile that the risk of talking the language of this culture, thinking its thoughts, trying to understand its points of view, is too great to be taken. Will not the faith be swept away and lost if we try to meet secular culture on its own ground? Yet if we are unwilling to do this, are we to live nostalgically in the past, as a kind of "remnant" that has survived into modern times but does not really belong here and can no longer have any influence or message?

It is very doubtful whether in our time there could be any grand synthesis such as Thomas Aquinas accomplished in the Middle Ages. Our own culture is not only more secularized, it is also more fragmented. There is no single dominant philosophy that speaks for the twentieth century. There are many conflicting philosophies and ideologies, and sometimes the conflicts are very sharp indeed. As we had occasion to note when we attempted to see what are the main characteristics of the secular outlook, we cannot say that secularism constitutes a philosophy. It is, rather, a mood that manifests itself in various philosophies, some of which conflict with one another. In this pluralistic world, the church has to conduct its apologetic on several fronts and must learn to communicate its faith in various ways, suited to the needs of different people. It may well be that in a culture so diverse and fragmented as that of the contemporary world, we cannot expect to find a way of talking of God that will make sense to everyone, but rather have to talk of him in a number of ways and in different conceptualities. Within the limits laid down by the gospel itself, the church must be prepared to become "all things to all men" (I Cor. 9:22). After all, no theology is final, and we could hardly suppose that in our time all the loose ends would be gathered up. So I think we may have to learn to live with a plurality of theologies, none of them perfect and none of them having a monopoly of the truth, but perhaps each of them able to speak with a special clarity to some given sector of contemporary society.

I do not think that such remarks push us toward an indifferentism, the view that one theology is as good as another (which, in fact, means that theology does not matter). But what we have been saying does push us toward a kind of relativism. There may be a number of "languages" available for talking about God and articulating the Christian faith today, and these may not all be mutually exclusive. Nevertheless, it is perhaps better to speak consistently in one language than to mix languages and come out with some weak kind of eclecticism. It may also be found in the end that there is some family likeness, so to speak, among the languages, for, as contemporary languages, it may well be that they will all share some features that stamp them as belonging to the world of today and distinguish them from the languages of an older time.

These languages which I have in mind are philosophical languages, bringing to expression the mentality of the contemporary epoch. There are, of course, other languages in which one can talk of God, such as psychological and sociological languages. These undoubtedly have their own usefulness, but they are inadequate to the theological task. The theologian has to talk of God not just as an idea in men's minds or as a cultural phenomenon but as the ontological reality on which Christian faith rests, and to talk of God in this way, he must enter the lists with the contemporary secular philosophers. It seems to me that one can distinguish three major types of philosophy in the contemporary secular culture, and one can correspondingly distinguish three major lines of exploration along which the theologians are seeking to express the reality of God for our time.

The first type of philosophy I want to mention is the kind that centers on such notions as "process," "evolution," "dynamism." Such philosophies have been rather prominent in the twentieth century, and one can mention such names as Samuel Alexander, Alfred North Whitehead, Charles Hartshorne, and in a somewhat different but related tradition, Henri Bergson. Through the last named, there is a relation also to the more empirically oriented school of William James and John Dewey. Perhaps all these men could be called "naturalists," though twentieth-century naturalism is a much richer kind of philosophy than the reductive naturalism (scarcely distinguishable from materialism) of the nineteenth century.

This twentieth-century naturalism or process philosophy does undoubtedly reflect many of the concerns of the secular outlook. As the very name "naturalism" implies, it takes for reality the world in space and time, whereas the older idealisms had tended to regard this world as simply "appearance." Again, these process philosophies have a profound respect for modern science, whether physics (Whitehead) or biology (Bergson). Above all, they lay stress on "becoming," so taking seriously the notions of time and development, as against philosophies that think of the real in terms of timeless, unchanging substance. One can also say that naturalism rejects dualism, and presumably this again reflects a secular point of view. In Daniel Day Williams' words, naturalism is "the *one-order theory of the world*. Everything that is concrete, everything that has actual power, whatever else it may be, is a structured spatio-temporal process."[3]

A philosophy that prizes science, takes time and becoming seriously, and speaks of a one-order world rather than of two worlds, undoubtedly takes care of most of the legitimate interests of the so-called secular outlook, and therefore affords a language in which Christian theology might seek to express itself. Many of the process philosophers, moreover, do not shirk the challenge of trying to bring together in one broad vision the multitudinous results of the separate sciences, and some of them, notably Whitehead and Hartshorne, have ended up with a theistic metaphysic, though admittedly their theism is different in some regards from the classic variety.

Thus it is not surprising that some Christian theologians have been attracted by these philosophies and have seen in them conceptualities for the articulation of Christian truth, especially of the doctrine of God, in a form that would speak intelligibly to the modern secularized mentality. This style of theology has been developed above all in the United States. Daniel D. Williams, Norman W. Pittenger, John B. Cobb, Schubert M. Ogden, and many others could be mentioned among its practitioners. Cobb rightly sees that Christian theology cannot get along without God, or make "God" simply a fancy name for the "depth" of my existence or something of the sort; and that the problem is "to try to restore the term 'God' to meaningful discourse in some real continuity with its historic use."[4] He himself tries to do this by way of a natural theology founded on Whitehead. After beginning with the world revealed to us by modern science, Whitehead tries to show that this world is best interpreted in terms of an idea of God that is also congruent with the Christian understanding of God. Schubert M. Ogden, in *The Reality of God,* to which we have alluded more than once, states: "It is my belief that the conceptuality provided by this new philosophy"—he has mentioned especially Whitehead and Hartshorne—"enables us so to conceive the reality of God that we may respect all that is legitimate in modern secularity, while also respecting fully the distinctive claims of Christian faith itself."[5]

In summary, this new-style theism which, according to Ogden, "in its scope and depth easily rivals the so-called *philosophia perennis,*" avoids the reductionism of earlier kinds of naturalism. This theism, beginning from the experienced world in all its concreteness and variety, claims that this reality cannot be interpreted in terms that fall below its own spiritual manifestations. This points to theism, but the difference between this "neoclassical" theism and older versions is that God is not now considered as a separate reality dwelling in timeless perfection apart from the world. In Daniel Day Williams' way of putting it: "There is an assertion that God and the world exist in a community of mutual action and passion. . . . We no longer try to think of God as unaffected by what happens among creatures, and perhaps with the mindbody analogy we can meaningfully conceive God's relationship to time and history."[6] Thus a relativity and a temporal aspect are introduced into the understanding of God. Yet he is not made just one object among others or absorbed into the world process. He is also accorded a uniqueness and "insurpassibility" that belong equally to his deity.

Along with these American versions of process theology I suppose we might reckon the immensely influential teachings of Pierre Teilhard de Chardin. His views, admittedly, have a more strongly biological and anthropological coloring, because of his special scientific interests. Nevertheless, his overall view of the cosmos as a directed process belongs within the same family as other evolutionary philosophies, and perhaps resembles most closely the emergent schemes of philosophers such as Conwy Lloyd Morgan and Samuel Alexander. Teilhard himself is philosophically weak, and there are considerable ambiguities in his thoughts of God. He is, in fact, caught between a traditional theism and a theism that would take more seriously the notions of temporality and becoming in relation to God.[7] Perhaps some of these difficulties in his theories can be overcome by his followers, especially through dialogue with the adherents of other kinds of process theology. What is perhaps most valuable in Teilhard's work is the style of prayer and spirituality that he developed, as, for example, in *Le Milieu Divin*.[8] Here we have, in an unusual combination, respect for science and for the material creation together with a lively sense of the divine Presence. When we recall what has been said on religion and spiritual discipline in an earlier chapter,[9] we can see that this particular contribution of Teilhard could be of great importance in the interpretation of the Christian faith in a secularized world. The misfortune is that it is backed up by such a poorly articulated philosophical and theological structure. On the other hand, it must be acknowledged that Teilhard's work seems to have spoken to at least some scientists, humanists, and even Marxists.

The second kind of philosophy that we see in the contemporary world is existentialism, including not only the accounts that this school of thought gives of human existence but also the ontologies that are built on an existential foundation. Martin Heidegger, Karl Jaspers, Jean-Paul Sartre are among the best known of the many exponents of existentialism. What is common to all these philosophers is that they take as their point of departure man's questioning of his own existence. Man himself in his concrete existing as a being-in-the-world is the point from which philosophical understanding must begin. But no human being is an isolated existent. The individual belongs in a community, the community in a history, and the history in a cosmos. In trying to answer the question of his own being, man finds himself driven to the ontological question of the wider being within which his being is set and apart from which it can be only an abstraction. The philosophers answer the questions about existence and being in various ways, but again we may say that this is a secular kind of philosophizing. It has moved away from dualism to the concreteness of being-in-the-world, and its categories, even for talking of the self and being, are temporal and historical rather than substantial and timeless. These philosophies may indeed be taken as typical expressions of the self-understanding of contemporary man. As such, they must clearly have first-class importance in any attempt to understand the mentality of this contemporary man and so in any attempt to interpret Christian faith, including faith in God, to him.

It seems to me that the theologians who have used the concepts of existentialism can be divided into two groups: those whose interest in existentialism has been confined mainly to its analysis of man in his historical existence, and those who have moved beyond this toward an existentially based ontology.

Rudolf Bultmann and his program of demythologizing afford the outstanding example of the first group, while closely related to him are Gogarten, Braun, and various others. This group has, in the main, drawn upon the existential analyses of Heidegger for its concepts of existence and history. And to protests that Christian theologians should not find it necessary to go to the "secularized" philosophy of Heidegger, Gogarten returns the perfect answer: "Needless to say, this truth does not have to be learned from Heidegger. If one thinks one can learn it better from another source, all well and good. But, in one way or another, learnt it must be."[10] One theologian who belongs in the same general area as those already mentioned in this paragraph but who has drawn his concepts from another source than Heidegger is Fritz Buri. His philosophical concepts come from Jaspers. Man in his freedom and responsibility, which he recognizes as gifts, recognizes his relation to a transcendence which he calls "God."[11]

But with this group of theologians the idea of God remains very elusive, as we have already noted in an earlier

mention of Bultmann and Gogarten.[12] If one can indeed
begin by exploring the contemporary secular man's self-
understanding, and can find in it areas that are open to
"transcendence" or to "God's acting" or whatever we may
call it, then a major step has certainly been taken toward
an interpretation, in the conceptuality of a secular philosophy, of the Christian faith in God. But much more clarity
has to be sought, and in particular one has to find some
ontological grounding for this God who is said to act on us
or to stir us up or to present us with our responsibility.

The second group of theologians within the existentialist camp consists of those who have in fact supported the
anthropological insights of existentialism with an ontology
that is likewise existentially based. As I have already said,
Tillich has made a signal contribution to a contemporary
understanding of God in terms of such an existentially
based ontology.[13] Bishop Robinson, so far as he has a consistent position, would seem to belong here too; but the
Bishop has also lent his support to views quite incompatible with this one, apparently feeling that any "new
theologian" who seems a bit far out must be doing something right.

I have tried to show elsewhere[14] that what I call "exis-
tential-ontological theism" develops an idea of God intelligible to the mind of today. It is "existential" because it
takes its departure from man's self-understanding, as analyzed and expounded in current philosophy. It finds man
to be concerned, whether explicitly or not, with the question of being—not with the question of another being
beyond the world (the discredited *deus ex machina* of
crude supernaturalism) but with the Being that is present
and manifest in the beings, that is to say, the beings that
constitute the world and of which man himself is one.
Insofar as man experiences this Being as holy, then he

rightly calls it "God." But neither man nor Being is "sub-stance," and to say this is simply to assert that they cannot be understood on the analogy of inert thinghood. They are constituted of temporality and of time, of history and of the letting-be of history. Here again, I would claim, we have a conception of God that concedes all the legitimate interests of the modern secular outlook.

We have still to consider a third type of contemporary philosophy. In the English-speaking countries, the tradi-tional empiricism is dominant, nowadays, in the form of logical empiricism. Whereas existentialism tends to be inward-looking, empiricism looks out on the world. It is the philosophy of common sense. It professes to deal in hard facts, not in speculations or in subjective attitudes. If it is to admit truth of any kind, then it looks for some kind of straightforward evidences. Above all, it admires the methods of the natural sciences, for they do seem to proceed in empirical ways and to arrive at solid and useful results. On the other hand, the empiricist is suspicious of any talk about God or any reality beyond the things that we can see and hear and handle.

Perhaps it is harder to express the meaning of Chris-tianity in terms that will reach the empiricist than it is to speak to the existentialist or to the process philosopher who is seeking a vision of reality as a whole. Both the exis-tentialist and the process philosopher are asking about the meaning of human life in the widest terms and thus they are open, to some extent, to a Christian answer. But the empiricist, absorbed in matters of fact, seems harder to reach. If he has become a positivist and will accept nothing that cannot be verified by sense experience, then, indeed, I doubt if he is open to any kind of God talk at all, or to any meaningful account of the Christian faith.

But few empiricists nowadays are dogmatic positivists,

and there is a broader tradition of empiricism, stemming from John Locke, that is by no means closed to such accounts of the Christian faith as can base themselves on human experience, understood in the broadest sense. Some Christian theologians believe that the church must learn to speak the language of the empiricists, must try to look at the facts as he looks at them, and must try to weigh the evidences that count with him.

A notable example of a Christian thinker who has worked along these lines is the Bishop of Durham, Dr. Ian T. Ramsey. In his best-known book, *Religious Language*,[15] he attempts "an empirical placing of theological phrases." Among other things, he seeks to show that if we do not understand "empiricism" in too narrow a sense, we can acknowledge that our experience of certain situations has a depth to it that he characterizes in terms of "discernment and commitment." It is in situations of this sort that religious language must be placed. He also explores what is involved in first-person language, and the logic of the models or analogues that are used in theological discourse.

While I have mentioned three major philosophical styles in which contemporary man expresses his outlook and how theologians are employing thought forms drawn from these types of philosophy, the divisions are by no means rigid, and some theologians draw on more than one philosophical style. I think one could also say that there are some things common to all three types, and perhaps these are the things which reflect the specifically "secular" mood of the time and which enable the theologian to present Christian faith in God in secular terms, so far as this is possible. Among these common features one would mention, first of all, the determination to take time and history seriously (and perhaps this is the essence of secularity);

second, a respect for the findings of natural science and for the scientific outlook; and, third, a refusal to subordinate the witness of everyday experience to some preconceived system of thought.

The theologians I have mentioned in this chapter have learned to talk the languages of the secular world, but this certainly does not mean that they have simply capitulated to secularism. Rather, they have tried to meet secular man where he is, believing that he is not really the self-sufficient person he is sometimes represented as being and that he can reach a true self-understanding only if there is opened up for him the lost dimension of the holy, and the reality of God.

All Christian apologetic implies risk, and probably some of the writers I have mentioned have fallen into errors of one kind or another. We certainly have to judge them critically, for if the secular outlook is taken to be a complete philosophy in itself, then it is futile to present Christ as relevant to a world that needs him no longer; if the gospel of technology is adequate to human needs, there is little point in putting a halo around it by identifying it with the gospel of Christ; and if God is irrelevant, there is not much sense in hanging on to some "reduced" version of Christianity. If secular man already has everything that he needs, Christianity should honestly confess that it has nothing to offer him. As Eric Mascall has seen, even Christian social theology is undermined if one has capitulated so much to the outlook of the secular world that no criterion is left for judging its worth.[16] The relation to contemporary thought must be a dialectical one. It is urgent that the church should speak to the secular man in his own language, but it is still more important that what the church speaks should be the authentic faith.

Chapter VII

The Reality of God

Underlying all the theological discussions about the place and significance of the secular is the fundamental question about the reality of God. I have made it clear that I do not think that Christianity, in any worthwhile form, could get along without a belief in God. Even the Christian's appreciation for the secular depends on the reality of God, for this appreciation is based on the doctrines of the creation and the incarnation. We have tried to show in earlier chapters that Christian theology can respond to the challenge of the contemporary world and that belief in God can be formulated in terms that respect whatever is valid in the secular outlook. But we are driven again to the question of God's reality. Even if some of the philosophical conceptions of God, adumbrated in the last chapter, are intellectually respectable, is the God whom they depict a reality, or do we need him? Are theologians simply exercising their ingenuity to keep a place for God, although we could get along very well without him, and perhaps the adult thing to do would be to thrust all thoughts of God behind us?

Certainly, a new wave of atheism has arisen in our time, and is making itself felt even within the Christian community. I call it a new wave of atheism, for it seems to have new motives, as compared with some of the older varieties of atheism. Of course, all atheism is relative to the kind of God that it denies. Just as theism has changed through the ages from mythological imagery through metaphysical speculation to the existential and historical thought forms of today, so atheism has had its development.

It may be that some factors remain constant in inclining some minds to atheism. An obvious example is the presence of evil in the world. To persons of any sensitivity, this constitutes a question mark opposite the name of God, and to some the fact of evil has seemed so massive and inexplicable that it has made belief in God impossible. This factor still operates today, especially with persons who have been exposed to some of the diabolical horrors and sufferings inflicted in this twentieth century.

Yet it seems to me that the principal motivation in contemporary atheism must be sought elsewhere. Contemporary atheism is not, after all, pessimistic, as it would be if it was mainly impressed with the evil of the world. It tends on the contrary to be optimistic—even extravagantly so. This is because, as it seems to me, it is motivated largely by man's self-assertion. It will be remembered that the last element mentioned in our analysis of the secular outlook was man's secular self-understanding, his sense of autonomy and of responsibility for his own destiny.[1] What could "faith" mean to such a person, especially faith in God? Would it not be a weakening of his own sense of responsibility? God begins to appear as the rival of man. Too long men have been subject to God or to the gods, and only as they learn to take matters into their own hands have they made any advance. So we are told that men cannot really be free to order their world and to build a better future for the race unless God is deposed and we take over complete responsibility ourselves.

It is clear then that this contemporary type of atheism is not based on, let us say, a materialistic metaphysic, as some older kinds of atheism were, but on man's desire to exercise that freedom which is part of his humanity. Although Marxism officially embraces a materialistic metaphysic, probably the Marxist critique of faith that is most influential nowadays is its view that religion is an anodyne preventing men from fulfilling themselves. Likewise, the Freudian critique treats belief in God as a neurosis, an immature attitude that ought to be discarded in a fully adult existence.

One is bound to recognize, therefore, that in contemporary atheism there are legitimate interests trying to find expression. If belief in God has been oppressive or immature, it is right to call such a belief in question. But surely the mistake of the atheist is his failure to recognize that man's concept of God can also grow and become increasingly mature. The legitimate criticism of false images of God can lead as well to more adequate ways of thinking of God, as was already happening long ago among Hebrew prophets and Greek philosophers alike.

Certainly the Christian, if he is theologically literate, would argue that the contemporary atheist has not understood who God is. He is no tyrant who keeps man in serfdom, but rather the very ground of his freedom and hope.

But not all Christians are saying this. A small number have opted for atheism. We have already said something of van Buren, but his rejection of God is based on a positivistic philosophy and is rather different from the kind of atheism we are now considering. It seems to me that the rejection of God in the name of human freedom—I might even say, in the name of a genuine humanity—is more typical of William Hamilton and Thomas Altizer.

These two men are themselves very different, and I think it is obviously Hamilton who is more representative of the contemporary mentality. Altizer[2] combines so many strands—mysticism, Orientalism, nineteenth-century German speculation, mythology, world affirmation, Christianity, and more besides—that it is very difficult to know what he is saying.[3] One of his favorite expressions is *coincidentia oppositorum,* and this really describes his own position. I myself suspect that his viewpoint is not so much an atheism as a paganism, in the line of Nietzsche. But then, how would one describe Nietzsche himself—nihilist, neopagan, or even some kind of Christian?

Some years ago, William Hamilton wrote a very fine little book entitled *The New Essence of Christianity.*[4] This book could, I think, be properly called "radical" theology, for it showed a very sensitive awareness of the precariousness of faith in the secular world and the elusiveness of God when we try to think of him in contemporary concepts. Hamiliton's point was that theologians should not set themselves up as persons having all the answers but that they should concentrate on the more modest task of trying to state clearly such essential truths of the Christian faith as we can grasp with reasonable assurance in the intellectual climate of our time. "This will mean living with very little theological security, in half-finished houses, with many things left unsaid because they are, for the moment, unsayable. This will mean running a real risk of robbing the Gospel of some of its power, or dishonestly putting forth a reduced Gospel so that modern man may be able to grasp it without so much difficulty."[5]

No one could find fault with what Hamilton is saying here, and every theologian in particular readily understands the problems that face him when he tries to meet honestly the challenges of modern thought. To use one of Hamilton's similes, the contemporary apologist is like a man trying to cover five windows with four storm windows. This reminds me of a verse in the Old Testament: "For the bed is too short to stretch oneself on it, and the covering too narrow to wrap oneself in it" (Isa. 28:20). I do not know what Isaiah had in mind when he wrote these words. One commentator says this was "a proverb for an intolerable situation which no expedient can remedy."[6] In any case, it seems to describe the situation of faith, for faith always has this vulnerability and insecurity. We try to make faith secure, but then it would no longer be faith, and we would also be rejecting the limitations and finitude that go with our human existence. When we think we have security, then we are probably deluding ourselves, having set up some dogmatic theism that brooks no question but which becomes stifling rather than creative in human life.

It seems to me that Hamilton (if I understand him aright) has moved from his radical and even poignant description of the situation of faith to a dogmatic atheism that is just as much a departure from the radical character of faith as is a dogmatic theism. How else does one interpret such a passage as: "It is not just that a capacity has dried up within us; we do not take all this as just a statement about our frail psyches, we take it as a statement about the nature of the world, and we try to convince others. God is dead."[7] And the motivation that has taken Hamilton in this direction seems clear enough. He calls it "Orestean theology." It aims at liberating man from God and from the struggle of faith. "To be freed from the parents is to be freed from religion, the religious *a priori*, religion as necessary, God as meeter of needs and solver of problems."[8]

But surely the contemporary revolt against God in the name of humanity is mistaken. Perhaps some gods have kept man in serfdom, and have tyrannized his life (though these would be better called demons, they are indeed distorted projections of the human mind itself). But is the true God like this? The very fact that we can talk of idols implies that there is a true God, who is no idol. For Christians, this is the God of the Bible, the God of Abraham, Isaac, and Jacob, the God and Father of Jesus Christ, the God of the church. This God, if we listen to the testimony of those who have believed in him, is no tyrant. He is rather the very ground of freedom and hope, the God through whom men have found themselves.

God, if we understand him aright, makes sense of our human life, and I doubt if we could make much sense of it apart from him. For what do we mean when we talk about "belief in God"? It means that we have faith in Being. By this, I do not just mean faith in my own being, or even faith in all humanity, but faith in that wider Being, in whom myself and all other men live and move and have our limited being. Belief in God is the faith that there is a context of meaning and value that transcends our human life, a context that we do not create and in which we already find ourselves. It is a context that makes sense of our human life, which would surely be a very problematic or even absurd phenomenon if we supposed that the wider being, wherein we have to live out our being, was either indifferent or hostile toward man and his aspirations.[9]

If we think of belief in God as this attitude of trust and

acceptance, we see that it is something much more than a metaphysical theory about the universe. It is the foundation for a whole "style of life," to borrow a phrase of which William Hamilton is fond, though other writers have used it too. Similarly, atheism is not just a theory that people can hold as a matter of indifference. Atheism too is a fundamental attitude toward life, held not only with the mind but expressing itself in character and action. The believer commits himself to Being that transcends his own being, Being that is not tyrannous but creative and that sets his life in a context of grace and judgment. The atheist, on the contrary, makes himself or human society the "measure of all things"; he neither looks for grace nor submits himself to judgment.

From some of the books being put out nowadays, one might conclude that atheism had proved its case and is the only possible belief for any educated and up-to-date person; whilst belief is a survival from the past, and is essentially immature. This is an utterly ridiculous and arrogant claim. I should say myself that theism is a much more *reasonable* belief than atheism and always has been. Whatever else one may say about natural theology, it at least, as John Courtney Murray points out,[10] takes a firm stand for the reasonableness of faith. The very fact that there is a world rather than just nothing, that this is an ordered and structured world rather than just chaos, and that this world has brought forth spiritual and personal beings, makes atheism a most improbable thesis.

On the other hand, it has to be acknowledged that this is an ambiguous world. If atheism is improbable, there are times when theism does not seem very probable either. In the face of suffering, waste, and apparent aimlessness, it is hard to believe in God or to have faith in Being—and obviously it is much harder for some people than for others. From ancient times, men have argued the case, some pointing to features that support theism and faith, others adducing evidence for atheism and unfaith. Although I have said that theism (in some form) is the more reasonable of the two beliefs, I do not think the arguments have ever been conclusive; by its very nature faith falls short of certitude and has its own vulnerability. The world remains ambiguous, and it is part of what it means to be a finite creature that we have to take our stand in this world and decide for faith or against it, without knowing in advance the answers to all our questions. Only in the end, the Christian believes, will faith be changed to sight.

I have tried to show in the preceding chapter how contemporary theologians are utilizing the insights and categories of current philosophies in order to speak of God in terms intelligible to our time. Criticisms of traditional theism are being met by the development of new forms of theism, and these in the long run will lead to a better and deeper understanding of Christian faith as a whole. Tillich, Hartshorne, Ogden, Herzog, Dewart—these are just a few of the names of men who, well aware of the inadequacies of traditional theism, are trying, in various ways and with varying degrees of success, to explicate the idea of God so that men today can know his reality.

But our faith, though we try to show that it is reasonable, is not first awakened by argument, nor does it primarily depend on philosophy. We believe in the midst of this ambiguous world because we have found in it a tradition of faith—a tradition that was there long before we appeared on the scene and will doubtless still be there long after we have left. The faith we hold had its origin among the Hebrew patriarchs, whose experience convinced them that a God of grace and judgment is present and active in the world. The faith was built up and sometimes severely tested through the centuries and found its culmination in Christ, the Word made flesh. The same faith has continued in the church, and millions are living by it today. For them, as for countless others in the past, this faith has helped to light up an ambiguous world, has made sense of some of its puzzles, and has offered a way of life that is both laid upon us as a demand and is at the same time supported and empowered by a grace that comes from beyond our little human resources. A faith that interprets the enigmas of life and that constantly expands and elevates the possibilities of human life, is surely no illusion but an utterly convincing reality.

Attempts to construct a version of Christian faith without God must be adjudged mistaken. There always have been people who have admired the Christian ethic and rejected the Christian faith, but ethic and faith are inseparable. The demand of the ethic can be endured only through divine grace, and grace has always seemed to me to be one of the most central elements in Christianity. I would agree with Leslie Dewart: "What is absolutely fundamental to the Christian experience is that which is conceptualized in the doctrine of grace."[11] Grace gets conceptualized in various ways by different theologians, but we can hardly think of it without God. So to say that the Christian ethic makes sense only in the context of a doctrine of grace is to say that it makes sense only in the context of a doctrine of God. But if the ethic cannot stand without faith, it must be equally denied that there can be any faith, properly so-called, that does not issue in the Christian ethic. "Faith by itself, if it has no works, is dead." (James 2:17.) Rather, it is not faith, but only an intellectual belief. It is not yet the commitment to and acceptance of Being that cannot fail to issue in a style of life.

However, if Christianity cannot be based on atheism, one must nevertheless acknowledge that the challenge of atheism is a constant safeguard against idolatry. Perhaps if Christians themselves permit the idea of God to become debased, then there is even justification for the appearance of an atheism within the Christian community. But this negative reaction could never, in the long run, be creative or even sustaining.

Idolatry arises when some image or concept of God gets absolutized, for no idea of God can be equal to the ineffable mystery of the reality. The current emphasis on depth as a symbol of God is, as we have already seen, well suited to the presentation of the idea of God in a secular age: to point to God in the depth of things and in the depth of our relations with each other. Yet this symbol must not be allowed to become absolute in turn. No single symbol of ours can contain God, and though he is in the depth, he is in the height as well. The height symbol refers to God's priority before all else, that he is the condition of everything that is, and of course this is an essential part of his deity. The old Celtic poets of Scotland were wiser than some of our modern apologists when they recognized God's presence above, below, and around them, in the things of nature and in the face of friend and stranger. Paul too was wiser when he spoke of the multidimensional way in which we must seek to think of God, and prayed that we "may have power to comprehend with all the saints what is the breadth and length and height and depth" (Eph. 3:18).

If there is justification for rejecting some of the distorted ideas of God that have sometimes been current in the church, nevertheless we can affirm that the full Biblical and Christian thought of God is one that the objections of the atheist do not reach. When the formal conceptions of God, derived from the philosophies considered in the preceding chapter, are filled out with the content derived from the Biblical revelation as transmitted in the community of faith, it seems to me that theism has a strong case indeed, and that many of the atheist's objections about the immaturity of faith are seen to be groundless. The theist is not committed to defending any and every idea of God, but the God who, as he believes, had made himself known in grace and judgment. Let me now fill out this thought of God.

First, we have to integrate into every new type of theism the Biblical thought of God. By exposing ourselves to the God of the Bible, we can be delivered from the constant temptation to domesticate God or to make him in our own images. We must, rather, stand before the God who has made himself known to us. I know of no more powerful exposition in a brief space of the essential character of the Biblical God than that provided by Jean Daniélou.[12] He sets out this character under the great qualities that are ascribed to God in the Old Testament. First, there is truth, the faithfulness and reliability of God that gives us the fundamental confidence for life; next, there is his justice or righteousness, the moral imperative that we find laid upon us and making an absolute claim on us; thirdly, there is his love or mercy, his positive building up of the life of his creatures; finally, there is his holiness, the mystery of God in his paradoxical strangeness and nearness. There is a world of meaning in every one of these qualities as they are developed in the Bible. They open to us something of the infinite riches of God, and show us how pitiably small our own ideas and images of God have been. But they show too how pitiably wrong the atheist is in some of the things he says about God. To believe in this God of the Bible is not immature or childish. He is no meeter of needs or solver of problems, but rather, as Daniélou says, "his ways disconcert us."[13] Such a God could never lull us into complacency, but is always drawing us beyond ourselves.

To the thought of the Biblical God, I would add next the classic idea of God as developed in Christian theology. This is the idea of the triune God. It is not just any God that the Christian believes in, but the God who has revealed himself as Father, Son, and Holy Spirit. It may well be that the language of "substance" and "persons" needs to be reinterpreted in the terminology of a more modern philosophy, and this is possible. But there can be no question of departing from the essential insight in the doctrine of God's triunity. This insight has, I should think, only a very tangential connection with the notion of "threeness." It is far more concerned to express the richness and complexity of the Christian understanding of God, which goes beyond any monolithic idea. Leslie Dewart expresses the matter well when he says of New Testament theism that "its ultimate basis must actually be considered not as the *unicity* of God but as the *self-communicating procession* of God."[14] My own way of expounding the triunity of God has been to see in this the movement of Being from its primordial source through its expression in creation to its unitive action in building up the Kingdom of God.[15] However we may try to conceptualize this mystery of the divine Being—and all our concepts must be inadequate to the reality—the meaning of the doctrine of God's triunity is plain enough. The doctrine speaks of that ceaselessly moving inner life of the Godhead, of that dynamic mystery which makes possible all life and love. This is what makes God the living God, as distinct from all the dead gods of history.

The last area on which we must draw for the strengthening and purifying of the idea of God is worship, the communing with God that is possible to man when he stands in God's presence. If God has become only a hypothesis, an abstract idea to be analyzed and argued about, then this is indeed a dead God. Men can only think truly about him if they have known his presence in the worshiping community. The living God is known as he is worshiped at his altars, and all true thinking about him is rooted in this meeting. But what then is this worship? We would sadly mistake Christian worship if we thought of it as some kind of homage paid to a superior power. We do not bow before an overwhelming *power,* but rather acknowledge an infinite *worth*—for "worship" is "worth-ship." Hence the service of God is not a servitude from which man, to be free and mature, must break loose. Rather, God's service is itself perfect freedom. This living God is rightly called love, for his letting-be or conferring of being is simply the ontological meaning of love. To worship God is to be conformed to his love and creativity, and so brought into a fuller humanity.

Thus I would argue that although the challenge of atheism in our time is a strong one, and although some of the atheist's points must be heeded as having a measure of justification, the challenge is, nevertheless, one that can be turned back. Theism is defensible philosophically, but, more importantly, when an abstract theism is filled out in terms of the Christian revelation of God, we can understand it as an utterly adult and fulfilling faith for contemporary man.

CHAPTER VIII

The Divine Attributes

We have tried to show that there are contemporary philosophies that allow us to construct ideas of God which are entirely compatible with those convictions to which we are committed in the scientific and technological age. We have tried to show further that these philosophical ideas of God are compatible with the Biblical teaching about God, and that it is indeed when we fill in the philosophical concept with the concrete Biblical testimony to God that we see we still have to deal with the living God of traditional Christian faith, and that even if we have nowadays to think in terms of new forms of theism, we are not inventing new gods.

Let us now test these assertions in another way, by considering some of the attributes of God. If God as he is conceived in the contemporary forms of theism is still the God of Abraham, Isaac, and Jacob, the God of Jesus Christ and of the Christian church, then we must expect that he will exhibit those attributes or fundamental characteristics which have been always ascribed to him. Perhaps we shall have to conceive of some of these attributes in different ways, but there would have to be a measure of continuity if we are to claim that we still believe in the God of the Bible and of Christian faith.

The first thing we must do is ask ourselves how we are to understand the word "attribute" in our talk about the attributes of God. The way of speaking suggests that the divine attributes, such as omniscience or incomprehensibility, are properties of God in a manner similar to the way in which rationality might be considered a property of man or flammability a property of gasoline. The next step might then seem to be that one would proceed to analyze these properties of omniscience and incomprehensibility in the same sort of way as one might seek to analyze such notions as rationality and flammability. But to do this would be to go on the assumption that God is an entity or a thing or a substance of some kind to which properties can be ascribed, and we have seen that a contemporary theism cannot think of him in this way. However we try to think of God nowadays, we can hardly suppose that he is another being in addition to the beings that we meet within the world. He is, rather, the *prius* of all such beings, the condition that there should be any particular beings at all. He is of a different order from all particular beings, though we meet him only in and through particular beings.

Hence, God does not fall under any of the regular categories of our thought, and so one must resist the tendency to suppose that one could analyze and exhibit the properties of God as one might do in the case of the properties of any particular being within the world. Admittedly, theologians, with their talk of "attributes" and with their overprecise attempts to give an account of these, have tended to encourage the idea that one can make an inventory and analysis of the divine characteristics. But the contemporary theologian would disavow any such intention. In recent theology it has been recognized that God cannot be objectified or submitted to the kind of scrutiny that would seem to be implied in the attempt to give a conceptual analysis of his "attributes." But even in the older styles of thought, there was always the tradition of negative theology that, if it did not impose silence, certainly stressed the inadequacy of our concepts in any discoursing about God and the need to take language about him in an indirect, symbolic way. So we must say first of all that the attributes are not properties that could be exactly analyzed or given a precise conceptual meaning, but rather symbols that point obliquely to some aspect or other of the mystery of God.

I think we must also say that there would be a shift in emphasis in any contemporary account of the attributes. Although we have seen that there are several secular philosophies current today that offer the possibility of understanding the world in a theistic way, we also took note that they have certain family resemblances.[1] Among these was the stress on history, becoming, process, time (and perhaps this is secularity in the strict sense). This would mean a shift away from such attributes as "immutability," which may have been apposite to God conceived of on the model of a thinglike substance, to more dynamic ways of thinking of God. Immutability would not be understood anymore as meaning a complete absence of change, but would be understood as a symbol pointing to the matchless stability and faithfulness of God while, on the other hand, it would be possible to think of the "living" God in a more realistic way than was possible when theology was dominated by the category of substantiality. A second characteristic that seemed to be shared by the various contemporary types of theism was their respect for the scientific investigation of the world and their consequent rejection of the old-style supernaturalism, insofar as it permitted arbitrary interferences in the course of nature. This would demand a new look at the divine attribute of "omnipotence," which certainly could not be understood as an absolute power to do anything.

Since we cannot study all the divine attributes, it may be worth our while to take this particular one, "omnipotence," and study it in more detail in the light of a contemporary theism. Before we get to the end of this study, however, we shall also say something about the attribute of love, for we have already noted that we do not worship God because of his power but because of his worth, and this is constituted primarily by his love.

It has been obvious for a long time that if one tries to take the idea of omnipotence as an exact concept, then all kinds of difficulties are encountered. If we try to analyze the concept of an absolute power to do anything, we find ourselves stumbling into all kinds of paradoxes and even downright contradictions. The classic criticism of the concept of omnipotence was provided at the beginning of the century by the philosopher John M. E. McTaggart,[2] and I think he made it clear that the attribution of a thoroughgoing omnipotence to God is something of which we cannot make sense nor can we reconcile it with other essential attributes of God.

Of course, long before McTaggart's time, theologians had been aware of some of the difficulties, and had tried to modify the concept of omnipotence in such ways as to overcome some of these difficulties. Anselm, for instance, had pointed out that God cannot lie,[3] for if he did so, this would be inconsistent with his nature and we could not properly call him "God." His freedom and power may, it is true, be unlimited in the sense that they are not subject to any external restraint, but they are subject to his own rationality, and so Anselm urges that they must be understood in a reasonable way. The point is well taken, so far as it goes. "Omnipotence" could hardly mean sheer unlimited capricious power that might break out in any direction—though it must be conceded that something like this idea occasionally appears in the Old Testament, as in the story of Uzzah and the Ark of the Covenant (II Sam. 6: 1–11). But God's power, though indeed mysterious, must be thought of as ordered or structured power, and as soon as we begin to think of it in this way, then we see that its very order or structure rules out any manifestations of it that would disrupt that structure.

But I am not going to pursue attempts to reach a satisfying theoretical conception that would be acceptable as an account of omnipotence. Admittedly, such attempts may have a logical and philosophical interest, but it seems to me that they miss the religious significance of omnipotence, and it is to this genuinely religious sense that we are pointed back by contemporary theism with its insistence that God is not a being or a substance but the mysterious Source of all beings, not itself falling under the categories that apply to the beings. In the religious language from which the word "omnipotence" comes and in which it has its home, so to speak, the word is an evocative image or symbol rather than a philosophical concept that can be precisely analyzed.

This actual Latinate word, "omnipotence," does indeed seem to belong to intellectualized and conceptualized ways of talking about God, but the history of the word shows that in its origins it had a fluid nonconceptual character. The word "omnipotent" actually occurs only once in the whole of the English Bible, in the Authorized (King

James) Version (Rev. 19:6). The corresponding word from Anglo-Saxon roots, "almighty," is fairly common in the Old Testament, but it occurs only nine times in the New Testament: eight of these occasions are in The Revelation, and the remaining one is a citation by Paul from the Old Testament. Certainly, then, one could not say that omnipotence is an important idea in the New Testament.

Moreover, the Hebrew word that is translated "almighty" in English versions of the Old Testament is *shaddai*. This is a word of uncertain significance, perhaps suggesting something like "exaltedness."[4] In any case, it did not convey any kind of developed concept of omnipotence. The Septuagint translated the word by *pantokratōr*, but the same expression was used to translate the phrase "of hosts," in the designation of the warrior God as the "Lord of hosts." I mention these points to show that in the Bible there is no precise concept of omnipotence, such as philosophers might argue over. The words translated "omnipotent" or "almighty" are used as symbols or pointers to indicate the mystery of the divine power and transcendence. This is just as true of the very restricted New Testament use of *pantokratōr* as it is of the Old Testament use of *shaddai*.

So the most basic religious and theological investigation into "omnipotence" would treat it as a symbol or image pointing to something that cannot be conceptualized, or, at any rate, adequately conceptualized. This kind of investigation comes before the logical and metaphysical puzzles encountered by scholastic theologians who did in fact try to conceptualize omnipotence. Yet we must say that the basic investigation into the mystery indicated by the word "omnipotence" is an ontological one.

In another writing,[5] I have attempted a rough classification of the divine attributes and I have there assigned omnipotence to the group that tries to express the *overwhelmingness* of God. By his overwhelmingness, I mean his ontological otherness, his difference from all particular beings, the numinous character that Rudolf Otto designated the *tremendum;* and to recognize something as having this character is, in Otto's words, "to mark it off by a feeling of peculiar dread, not to be mistaken for any ordinary dread, that is, to appraise it by the category of the numinous."[6] Most of the words used to express the overwhelmingness of God are negative words. The otherness of God, which cannot be brought within the everyday categories or analyzed in the concepts at our disposal, is hinted at in the negative theology. This proceeds by denying that God is limited by the characteristics that belong to particular beings or that he can be measured by the standards that belong to such beings.

But all negative theology has some positive content, and this arises from developing the contrast between the negative expression and its opposite, as we know the latter in ordinary experience. For instance, the negative expression "infinite" is understood in relation to what we mean by "finite." It is indeed possible to try to construct a concept of the infinite, perhaps by calling in the aid of mathematics and physics, but whether any such speculative idea of infinity has much relevance to the theological understanding of God seems to me very doubtful. As applied to God, the word "infinite" is contrasted with the felt finitude of a human existence, and the basic sense of the word in a theological or religious context is to be sought by developing the contrast between the existentially grasped sense of finitude on the one hand and the overwhelmingness of God on the other.

Although the expression "omnipotent" is not a negative one—it might even seem to lie at the opposite extreme from negation— we must try to elicit its meaning in a way similar to that in which one must try to elucidate the expressions of negative theology. To speak of "omnipotence" or "almightiness" is to suggest a power or capacity that is opposite in its characteristics from the powers and capacities of man and, in particular, that is not bound by the kind of limitations that pertain to the exercise of human power. Omnipotence is a power characterized by otherness and overwhelmingness. Any attempt to understand what this might mean must set out from the awareness of power and energy that we have at first hand in our own human existing. Then, by developing certain contrasts, we may be able to move from the existential understanding of power that belongs to us as agents who exercise power, to an ontological understanding, however shadowy and approximate it may be, of the overwhelming power of that Being by virture of which and within which our particular beings have to exist.

Here I shall introduce some interesting observations on power from the work of Martin Heidegger.[7] Seizing on the Greek tragedian's description of man as *to deinotaton* (the "strangest" or the "most terrible"), Heidegger claims that "this one word encompasses the extreme limits and abrupt abysses of his being." As Heidegger interprets the Greek word, it points primarily to "overpowering power," and, concerning man, he can say that "the use of power is the basic trait not only of his action but also of his being-there." But this exercise of power by man takes place in the midst of the overwhelming power to which man is exposed in the world, and the world itself gets shaped in both the conflict and the co-working of these two manifestations of power.

Let us now see whether we can develop more clearly the contrast between the power that man knows in his own existence and the power that he ascribes to God. There are especially two ways in which these manifestations of power may be opposed, so that there is brought out the otherness or overwhelmingness of the divine power.

The first contrast has to do with the point that man's power is always the power of one particular being in relation to other particular beings. Such power may shape and control, may bind and liberate, but it never absolutely creates or destroys. On the other hand, it is precisely absolute creativity that belongs to the divine power, for God is not another particular being but rather Being itself, the letting-be in virtue of which all particular beings are. He is not another being but—if we may for a moment borrow an expression from the language of Paul Tillich—the power of being in everything that is.[8] This is not an altogether happy expression, and is capable of more than one interpretation, but it may be used to point to something that is quite uniquely characteristic of divine power—the power to stand out from nothing and to *be,* or perhaps one should say, rather, the power to let something stand out from nothing and to be (*creatio ex nihilo*). This overwhelming power, completely other than any human exercise of power, may be considered as one basic strand in what we mean by "omnipotence" or "almightiness."

The second contrast arises from the fact that man is always a being-there, a being that already finds itself in a particular situation as one that has already been, so that what remains open in that situation is always limited by the many givens of the situation. This may be expressed in another way by saying that the possibilities of human existence are always conditioned by the factical circumstances of a concrete situation. Any human existence finds itself thrown into the stream of history and becoming, and occupying a given point in that stream. But if God is not a particular being, then we cannot think of him as a being-there, or as one whose possibilities are limited by a factical situation. Rather, his possibilities would not be tied to any particular situation, and perhaps this transcending of all particular situations and perspectives could be the basis for a providential activity on the part of God.

It may be claimed that the two ways of approaching an interpretation of divine power that have just been sketched out do in fact point to something so completely transcending the human power of our everyday experience that we might well feel justified in calling it "omnipotence" or "almightiness." But it is also clear that this mysterious overwhelming powerfulness has nothing to do with an arbitrary or capricious power that might manifest itself in magical or irrational happenings. This was excluded from the start by the existential approach to the question about the meaning of "omnipotence." The model from which we set out was not power as we can observe it in nature, but power as we know it in our own human existence as exercisers of power. This human power, manifesting itself in *action,* has a unity and structure about it that does not belong to the sheer *energy* of nature, though clearly even this is not without some structure and order. Presumably, the power of God would be even more a power characterized by structure, direction, and order; and indeed it would have these characteristics to an extent far beyond what we can see in either the rational power of human action or the organic power of natural energy.

But this point must be pursued further. While we have followed the custom of talking about the "attributes" of

God, we have agreed that these cannot be regarded as if they were like the properties of some particular being. This means that while we may, for the sake of convenience, isolate some particular attribute for discussion, we must remember that it belongs together with all the others in the unity of the divine Being. Puzzles and antinomies arise when we wrongly abstract some single one of the attributes of God, seize upon it in isolation, interpret it in an over-literal and conceptualized way, and then complain that it conflicts with other attributes, likewise considered in abstraction.

The conflict most relevant to our present discussion is the one that is supposed to arise between God's omnipotence and his love or mercy. It is often said that if God is omnipotent, he cannot be loving, for he would not permit evil in the world; while, if he is loving, he cannot be omnipotent and must be unable to prevent evil.

But from what we have already seen, we must say that God's omnipotence and his love are simply different ways of pointing to the one fundamental character of God—his creativity, his unique and mysterious letting-be of the beings. It was this letting-be that impressed us as the most absolute kind of power, and the kind that is most "other" than what we know in our human experience of power. But it is also letting-be, the conferring of being, that is the highest form of love.[9] Omnipotence and love are different aspects of the one fundamental divine activity of letting-be the particular beings of the world.

This helps to explain how it happens that if we try to conceptualize in too precise a manner any single one of the divine attributes, we run into paradox, if not into sheer contradiction. Our only safeguard against this is to acknowledge that these attributes have an approximate and symbolic character, as pointing to something that escapes conceptualization in the categories of our everyday thought; and that therefore each symbol must always be held together with others, which correct it. This in effect means that these symbols, like all analogues, must be held dialectically, and at once affirmed and denied.[10]

In the case of omnipotence, we may say that an absolute power is evidenced in the creative act of bringing into being, or letting be; yet this very act in itself constitutes a limit to power, for the primordial Being has, so to speak, poured itself out, and so exposed itself to the risks inherent in a world of particular beings, and thus of conflicting powers. The highest manifestation of an absolute power would be the bringing forth of such beings as man himself, beings that possess a limited creativity and power to let be; yet this highest manifestation of power is also the division of power, the sharing and surrendering of a measure of power, so that over against the overwhelming power is now set the power of man—let us remember that Sophocles called him *"to deinotaton"*—a power that may either conflict or cooperate with the universal power.

One could say very much the same things from a different starting point, setting out from love as another aspect of letting-be. For we could say that the highest act of love is the creative act of letting another be, of conferring being upon him, of enabling him to become what he authentically is; yet this very act implies separation and the breakup of union, with the potentiality for conflict.

So in both cases, whether we consider the primordial letting-be as omnipotence or love, there is a tragic side to it, and it would appear that evil is inevitable in creation. But this also means that any theological doctrine of creation is inseparable from a doctrine of reconciliation.

The fundamental paradox finds expression in the Christian symbol of the cross, where power and suffering, exaltation and humiliation, are presented together. God shows his absolute power and love by sharing in the sufferings of his creation, though one may also hope that this is a redemptive sharing that leads to a new creation.

Probably the word "omnipotent" (and the same might be said about some other attribute words) is far too artificial and metaphysical an expression to stand for the mystery of the God who lets the world be. It is a word that needs to be interpreted in some concretely religious and theological way, such as has been attempted here. But this procedure also helps to link our contemporary theism more firmly with the Biblical tradition, for behind this word "omnipotent" is the tradition of faith that stretches back to *El shaddai,* the primordial power of Being that was felt rather than conceptualized as soon as men began to ask about their own existence.

Chapter IX

God's Presence and Manifestation

It is time for us to gather together the reflections in which we have been engaged in the course of this book. Our problem has been that of God in a secular age—the problem of how to understand him in the context of secularity and perhaps, too, the problem of how to realize his presence. We began from the apparent opposition of God and secularity, as the two poles within which the current theological discussion moves. We have considered some of the many strands that make up contemporary theology, especially some of the versions of a "secular" Christianity. We have tried to do this both sympathetically and critically, so that we might sort out the truth and the error. It must certainly be acknowledged, and we have seen good reason to believe, that Christian truths are trying to find expression in the theological movements of our time; but it has likewise become clear to us that there have been exaggerations and distortions, and that as new truths are discovered (or rediscovered), equally important truths tend to get forgotten. Perhaps it just is the fate of theology to swing to one-sided extremes and never to attain to the tension of a true dialectic. There is today an understandable reaction against the whole movement that we associate chiefly with Karl Barth, but it would be sad indeed if we just went back to unreconstructed liberalism, as if Schweitzer and Barth and Niebuhr and the rest had never lived, as if we had never heard of sin and judgment and transcendence and eschatology, or at least had reduced these to harmless symbols.

Error occurs whenever a half-truth gets passed off as if it were the whole truth, for then it becomes a perversion. We have seen several instances of this. We have seen how the truth that otherworldly concerns can make people indifferent to conditions in this world is perverted to the view that only the tangible and the material are of any importance. We have seen how the truth that man has freedom and responsibility gets distorted into the utterly erroneous and unbiblical assertion that he is entirely self-sufficient and autonomous. We have seen how the truth that religion can become an anodyne is changed into the absurdity of "religionless" Christianity and into an attack on prayer, worship, and devotion. We have seen, finally, how the truth that our ideas of God have often degenerated to the level of the infantile and the unworthy has been made the excuse for an attack on all belief in God, in the name of a Christian atheism. All these excesses must be criticized and corrected.

But errors and heresies arise in the church because the half-truths that they contain have been neglected in the church's own teaching. It is for this reason that some writers have held, with some justification, that even Marxism could be considered a Christian heresy. Broken off from the whole and leading a life of its own, it has indeed become dangerous and distorted, yet in some cases at least it may be witnessing to social values that the official church has allowed to become forgotten. This does not mean that the Christian is to condone Marxism or the extravagances of contemporary theologians who, like the Marxists, may have seized on forgotten truths but have then pursued these in one-sided and distorted ways. In all such cases, we have to acknowledge that these people have been driven to their exaggerations because the church has been slow to come to terms either with the science and philosophy of modern times or with the changes that are going on in modern society. It has understressed elements in the Biblical and Christian tradition that are relevant to the situation of our times, and so it must not be surprised when these things assert themselves with an explosive violence that may seem very threatening.

If these remarks have any measure of truth, then the correct procedure for the church in face of the new theological movements of today is not to condemn them or merely to fight against them, but rather to set what is true and wholesome within them in the wider context of the entire Christian faith. The half-truths that can become downright errors when taught in isolation are given their due when they are presented as part of the whole Christian faith; and the whole faith is thereby enriched as it is appreciated in a more dialectical way and its many bearings on human life are allowed to work in balance and tension. Indeed, it is only within the organic fullness of the whole faith that any Christian truths can become really effective in the lives of men and can bring forth the fruits of the Spirit. This is most certainly the case as regards whatever elements of truth there are in the various "secular" presentations of the gospel. In isolation, some of these elements would have to be judged not only erroneous but also as tending toward harmful practical attitudes among those who adhere to them. What I have in mind is that Christianity allows itself to be absorbed into a secular culture that is, in fact, very far from possessing all the desirable qualities that some of our idealistic secularizing theologians attribute to it. The crucial question here is well expressed by John Bennett: "Is there not a serious danger that the Church's mission may become lost in the world? And must we not once again stress the independence of the Church's own base, its transcendence of the world?"[1]

A right attitude to the secular (from a Christian point of view) and a right use and appreciation of the material world depend on seeing these in the perspective of the whole faith. Since that whole faith centers in God himself, what we are saying is that our understanding has to be broad enough so that it takes in the two poles from which our discussion set out—God and secularity; and that it tries to see these in the unity of the Christian faith, especially by developing those doctrines of the faith which specifically link God with the material world. I have already indicated various ways in which the truths contained in the so-called "new" theologies can be rescued from the distortions that threaten them and be used for the enrichment of our understanding of Christianity in its relevance to our time. However, I shall now mention five specific Christian doctrines that seem to me to be of first-class importance in constructing that total Christian vision that will do justice to the secular without diminishing the centrality of God in Christian faith. These doctrines are basic in any attempt to sketch out a theology of the secular. If we try to set our understanding of these matters within this broadly based framework, I think we shall be in less danger of falling into distortions. We shall not be in danger of despising the secular, but, equally, we may hope to escape some of the foolish excesses into which uncritical champions of the secular have run.

The first of the five doctrines is the doctrine of creation. "God saw everything that he had made, and behold, it was very good." (Gen. 1:31.) This doctrine separates Biblical faith from Gnosticism, Manichaeism, Puritanism, and every other view that condemns the material and the fleshly as somehow inherently evil. The world, as God's creation, has its place in his good purpose, and is meant for our use and enjoyment, for the fulfillment and expansion of our lives. For God, if we may so speak, has not been content to be an eremite (which indeed he never was) but has shared being with his creatures. Creation comes from the overflowing of his love and creativity, and something of himself goes into the world. That it has its origin in the divine goodness is the charter of the world and of the history enacted in it. The potentialities of creation have more and more unfolded until at last spiritual beings (existents) have been brought forth, able to direct their lives and to assume responsibility for them.

Yet this same doctrine of creation, which affirms the basic goodness of matter, the world, creaturely being, history—in a word, the secular—is unintelligible apart from the thought of the transcendent Creator. We cannot allow to fall out of sight God himself, the prior condition of there being any creatures whatsoever. The world does not exist of itself, and it is not an ultimate. To understand its significance, we have to see it in its relation to God, who has brought it into being. We go wrong if we put it in God's place or prize it as something complete in itself. This would be the distortion of secularity into secularism if anyone wants to make that particular distinction.

More than this, the doctrine of creation declares that this is God's world, not ours. We are the guardians of the world, or rather of our little corner of a world that is inconceivably vast in space and time. A guardian is a steward rather than a master or owner. Thus man's use and exploitation of the world must be controlled by the remembrance that we too are creatures of God, that we too owe our being to him and live in the presence of his grace and judgment, so that a heavy responsibility lies on us.

The second doctrine to be borne in mind is the doctrine of the incarnation, the very center of the Christian faith. "The Word became flesh and dwelt among us, full of grace and truth." (John 1:14.) The church fathers were right in linking the doctrines of creation and incarnation, and in thinking of the incarnation as a kind of "recapitulation" of creation. It is as if the incarnation focuses in a single point what God has, in a sense, been doing always and everywhere; and if, in an ambiguous world, God's presence and action are often hidden, the Christian claim is that he is signally present and manifest in Jesus Christ, the incarnate Word, so that Christ becomes the center for the interpretation of the whole.

If, as we have already suggested, God has put something of himself into the creation and has exposed himself to the risks of a creation that has potentialities for development toward responsibility and freedom, these points are made manifest in the incarnation. In this event, we claim, God has come right into the midst of time and history in an embodied existence; the original creativity and self-giving of God expressed in the doctrine of creation are in Christ more plainly manifested in a life of creativity and self-giving, so that we are bound to call this life divine as well as human. In this incarnate life is declared, just about as clearly as it possibly could be, God's concern for his world and what goes on in it.

And let us remember that the church has always fought

against any docetic view of the incarnation, as if Jesus Christ just "appeared" as a man, and did not really share our humanity. He did indeed live *in the flesh,* knowing its weariness, pain, and temptation, and caring for the daily down-to-earth needs of the men and women among whom he lived. The incarnation declares that God has become present and manifest in the flesh.

We move on without a break to the third doctrine, the doctrine of the church, "which is his body, the fulness of him who fills all in all" (Eph. 1:23). God summed up the meaning of creation in a human person, Jesus Christ; but no human person is an island, for what is involved in being human implies, among other things, a being-with, a community with other existents; thus Christ cannot be separated from the social reality of which he was the center. This social reality we call his body. In the first instance it is the church, but ideally it is all humanity. I do not believe that this intimate relation of Christology and ecclesiology is anywhere better set forth than it has been by John Knox, in a manner that is truly radical and yet profoundly catholic.[2]

We must affirm, then, that God is present and manifest in the human social reality of the church. At first sight, this may seem an arrogant claim, and no doubt it has often been misunderstood by the church itself in ways that have led to arrogance. Yet the claim must be made if the church is the body of Christ and partakes of his nature. To say that God is present and manifest in the church is to affirm that "transcendence of the world," which, as we have seen, John Bennett ascribes to the church and holds to be essential to its mission in secular society.[3] In the depth of its being, the church is a community of faith responsive to God in Christ. Yet the church is also a fully human society

that can work only through social and institutional structures. In its doctrine of the church, the Christian faith is
again declaring, as in the doctrines of creation and incarnation, that it is only through earthy entities and structures
that God becomes present and manifest—and if he were
not present and manifest, he could hardly be called God at
all. Yet this recognition of the place of structures and
institutions reminds us once more of the emptiness and
futility, as well as the essential docetism, of so-called "religionless" Christianity. Christianity without a body could
be only a ghost. As creatures of flesh and blood, we do not
know God immediately in his pure spiritual glory, but
only through the medium of things that are very earthy,
human, and secular.

I said that the claims made for the church are only
arrogant if they are misunderstood. They are misunderstood if we think of the church as some specially favored
group, called out from the mass of mankind to enjoy
special privileges. Perhaps the doctrine of election has
sometimes been understood in this way, or rather, we
should say, misunderstood. The church is certainly called
of God—this is implicit in the very word *ekklēsia*. But the
call is directed to all men, all men are embraced in God's
saving work and are ideally included in the community
of faith that came into being with the incarnation, or even
with the creation itself. The border between the church
and the "world" is always a fluid one. The church is not a
privileged group that has been rescued from the world, as
it were, but is, rather, that part of humanity which has
been charged with a special responsibility toward all humanity—the responsibility of sharing in God's creative
and reconciling work and of leading the human race into
the ever fuller existence that God has set before it.

This brings us to the fourth doctrine—the doctrine of sacramental presence. "The Lord Jesus on the night when he was betrayed took bread, and when he had given thanks, he broke it, and said, 'This is my body which is for you.'" (I Cor. 11:23–24.) God becomes our food. This statement, made so bluntly, might seem almost blasphemous, and presumably it would seem so to anyone for whom the words "faith" and "religion" refer to supposedly purely spiritual realities. But the words are not blasphemous in the context of the Christian faith, and in the light of all the ways in which that faith links together God and secularity, the mysterious creative source from which everything has its being, and that multiplicity of finite and creaturely beings themselves.

God, of course, can be present in many ways. He can undoubtedly be present in his word, and it is this "word presence" that Protestantism has chiefly stressed. Catholicism, on the other hand, has stressed God's sacramental presence especially in the physical elements of the Eucharist, and perhaps this sacramental presence expresses in a more vivid and meaningful way the closeness of God to his created world. Ideally, however, the two modes of presence, sacramental and evangelical, should not be separated, and probably there is a growing realization of this among both Protestants and Catholics.

Surely sacramental devotion makes a vast difference in the way in which persons perceive their world. The sacrament of the altar, like the incarnation itself, which it re-presents, becomes a focus of interpretation for the material world as a whole. This is seen as a sacramental world that has become transparent to the God who has made it and put himself in it. Anything can be a sacrament, from nature as poetic souls experience it to the neighbor, the nearest "thou" who, as Buber has it, is "a glimpse through to the eternal Thou."[4]

The type of Christian faith that has stressed the sacraments and has usually also had room for some kind of natural theology has never regarded the world as evil in the way that some varieties of Puritanism and Protestantism have done, and thus does not need to make the violent overcorrection to be observed among those Protestant theologians who have become so enthusiastic over their newfound love of the secular. Anglicans in the tradition of Maurice, Gore, and Temple must be wondering what all the fuss is about.

The last doctrine to be considered is eschatology. This is the belief that there is a directedness in the world process and that it moves on into fuller being. I cannot agree with Leslie Dewart's belief that, because of his freedom, man might thwart this movement and end up in a real irreversible hell.[5] I do not think it is inconsistent to say on the one hand that man's free cooperation is indispensable to the advance of God's Kingdom, and yet to affirm on the other hand that there is a dialectic in history whereby God too is working, and that he is moreover always a step ahead so that even man's follies and sins are transmuted. This indeed is surely an important part of the meaning of Christ's cross and resurrection.

The theological "virtue" connected with eschatology is hope. This hope believes that nothing can be so mean or "profane," nothing even can be so wicked, that it cannot somehow be worked upon by God's redemptive and creative love and that it cannot finally serve his purpose.

It is within the framework of these great doctrines of the Christian faith that the true interests of secularity will, in the long run, be best safeguarded. The shortsighted secularism that fastens attention only on the immanent realities of the world can all too easily become an inhuman ideology. We must claim then that a true appreciation for the secular demands that we have also a true understanding of God. New ways of conceptualizing God are certainly called for, and we have seen how theologians are at work on the problem of finding suitable concepts. But although we may have new forms of theism, this does not mean we shall have new gods. Rather, we may hope to gain deeper understanding of the God who has been from the beginning. He is the God who created the world, conferring not only being but dignity and meaning upon it; he is the God who put himself into the world and still does so; he is the God who—such is our hope—leads both men and all his other creatures into ever fuller being.

Guide to Recent Literature on the Problem of God

The background of the present discussion is to be found in the works of the theologians of the last generation— Barth, Tillich, Bultmann, Bonhoeffer, Gogarten, and others; and, behind them, in the philosophy and theology of the nineteenth century and earlier. However, the following list is confined to the more important books on the question of God that have been published in the past five years or so. They are listed approximately in chronological order, and anyone wishing to be conversant with the debate about God should read through these books in the order shown. But for those coming late to this debate, this might mean too much catching up and might be too time-consuming. So I have suggested four shorter schemes of reading, with six books in each. These schemes are indicated by the letter A, B, C, or D placed before the title of each book. Each scheme has been selected to give a balanced picture of the debate, with opposing points of view represented; and where possible, the selection has been made so that the earlier books in each scheme are criticized in the later ones. Scheme D is the most philosophically-oriented of the four. An introduction to some of the leading personalities in the debate is given in Ved Mehta's

The New Theologian (Harper & Row, Publishers, Inc., 1966).

A. *The Death of God,* by Gabriel Vahanian. George Braziller, Inc., 1961. 253 pp. This is a historical and cultural analysis, designed to show how our post-Christian world is based on the assumption of the death of God. Hostile to every kind of religiosity and idolatry, the book seems to leave room for a genuinely transcendent God before whom man can be free.

B. *The New Essence of Christianity,* by William Hamilton. Association Press, 1961; 2d ed., 1966. 159 pp. A sensitive book in which the author frankly faces the difficulties of belief in our time, and proposes that the Christian should concentrate on those essentials of the faith of which he can be sure. Hamilton's ethical and pragmatic interests are apparent, but in this book he has not yet reached his more negative conclusions about the "death of God."

C. *Honest to God,* by John A. T. Robinson. London: SCM Press, Ltd., 1963; The Westminster Press, 1963. 143 pp. If we remember that this book had a "tentative and exploratory" character, we can acknowledge its value in popularizing the views of Tillich, Bultmann, and Bonhoeffer, and in getting the present debate about God started. The fantastic sales of this book show that the question of God is by no means a dead issue.

C. *The Honest to God Debate,* edited by D. L. Edwards. London: SCM Press, Ltd., 1963; The Westminster Press, 1963. 287 pp. The reaction to Bishop Robinson's book. Letters, reviews, and articles take up the problem of God as the Bishop had raised it. He furnishes a reply to his critics.

A. *The Secular Meaning of the Gospel,* by Paul M. van Buren. The Macmillan Company, 1963. 205 pp. The clearest and most philosophical presentation of a "secular" Christianity, based on the methods of British logical analysis. The author believes that all reference to a transcendent God must be eliminated, and Christianity "reduced" within ethical and historical dimensions.

C. *The Existence of God as Confessed by Faith,* by Helmut Gollwitzer. The Westminster Press, 1964. 256 pp. A Continental contribution. There is searching criticism of the extreme Bultmannians and also of Bishop Robinson. The author's affirmative argument is weak, being dependent on appeal to special revelation.

A. *The Problem of God: Yesterday and Today,* by John Courtney Murray, S.J. Yale University Press, 1964. 121 pp. An excellent example of contemporary Roman Catholic thinking. Clearly written and backed by impressive learning, the book shows that the Biblical and theological understandings of God are by no means superseded. There is a perceptive analysis of modern and "postmodern" atheism.

D. *The Search for God,* by Robert W. Gleason, S.J. Sheed & Ward, Inc., 1964. 311 pp. Another solid piece of Roman Catholic scholarship. The book explores both contemporary and traditional philosophical thinking about God, and links this with the Biblical understanding of God.

D. *The God We Seek,* by Paul Weiss. Southern Illinois University Press, 1964. 258 pp. This is a discussion of the problem of God from the viewpoint of philosophy rather than of religion. Leaving aside appeals to special revelations, the author distinguishes fifteen approaches to God from human thought and experience.

B. *The Real God,* by Alfred B. Starratt. The Westminster Press, 1965. 124 pp. The interest of this book lies not so much in its sketch of an idea of God (an idea that tends toward pantheism) as in its relating the problem of God to the practical issues of the pastoral ministry.

D. *Belief and Unbelief,* by Michael Novak. The Macmillan Company, 1965. 223 pp. A frank and able discussion by a young Roman Catholic philosopher. He finds a basis for belief in self-knowledge, and especially in his concept of "intelligent subjectivity."

B. *The Secular City,* by Harvey Cox. The Macmillan Company, 1965. 276 pp. This best-selling book is only tangentially concerned with the problem of God, but it is included here because it has been so influential in promoting a new and more appreciative Christian attitude to the secular.

C. *Sacred and Secular,* by A. M. Ramsey. London: SCM Press, Ltd., 1965; Harper & Row, Publishers, Inc., 1965. 83 pp. In this short book, the Archbishop of Canterbury shows how Christian faith is constituted by a dialectic of worldly and otherworldly.

C. *The Rock and the River,* by Martin Thornton. London: Hodder & Stoughton, Ltd., 1965; Morehouse-Barlow Co., 1965. 158 pp. An unusual and important book. Thornton considers how one goes from faith to ethics, and shows the need, neglected in much of the new theology, for a spiritual discipline.

D. *A Christian Natural Theology: Based on the Thought of Alfred North Whitehead,* by John B. Cobb, Jr. The Westminster Press, 1965. 288 pp. The author believes that Whitehead's philosophical understanding of God offers the basis for a Christian natural theology, and most of the book is taken up with a clear exposition of Whitehead's views.

C. *The Secularization of the Gospel,* by Eric L. Mascall. London: Darton, Longman & Todd, Ltd., 1965; Holt,

Rinehart & Winston, Inc., 1966. 286 pp. A penetrating but somewhat ponderous criticism of Robinson and van Buren by one of England's leading theologians. It shows up many weaknesses and superficialities, especially in Robinson, but lacks sympathy for the contemporary mentality.

B. *Radical Theology and the Death of God,* by Thomas J. J. Altizer and William Hamilton. The Bobbs-Merrill Company, Inc., 1966. 202 pp. A kind of sourcebook for the extreme wing of the "death of God" movement. It contains essays written for journals over the past few years. The book shows how Hamilton's views have developed in an atheistic direction, and affords an introduction to Altizer.

B. *The Gospel of Christian Atheism,* by Thomas J. J. Altizer. The Westminster Press, 1966. 157 pp. Altizer offers his clearest and most definitive statement to date. In his view, God died at a definite time in history. His thought is a compound of Eastern mysticism, nineteenth-century German philosophy (especially Nietzsche), and other items.

A. *The Next Christian Epoch,* by Arthur A. Vogel. Harper & Row, Publishers, Inc., 1966. 111 pp. The author sees no future for Christianity if God is dead: "If you cut off a chicken's head, it may run round the yard two or three times before dropping!" But through a phenomenological analysis of man's being-in-the-world, Vogel builds a case for a contemporary restatement of Christian faith that will be loyal to the essential tradition.

A. *Secular Christianity,* by Ronald Gregor Smith. London: William Collins Sons & Co., Ltd., 1966; Harper & Row, Publishers, Inc., 1966. 222 pp. This Scottish theologian bases his work mainly on Bultmann and Bonhoeffer. By a "secular" Christianity, he means one that is expressed in historical categories, but he does not deny a transcendence that meets man in history.

A. *The Reality of God,* by Schubert M. Ogden. Harper & Row, Publishers, Inc., 1966. 237 pp. Acknowledging that traditional theism is in trouble, but holding that Christian faith without God is an absurdity, the author seeks to develop a neoclassical theism on the basis of process philosophy. The best and most serious book on God to appear in the past five years.

D. *Understanding God,* by Frederick Herzog. Charles Scribner's Sons, 1966. 191 pp. A thoughtful and constructive book, which has the great merit of linking the debate about God to other theological concerns of our time, especially the "new hermeneutic."

D. *The Future of Belief: Theism in a World Come of Age,* by Leslie Dewart. Herder & Herder, Inc., 1966. 223 pp. Like Ogden, this Roman Catholic writer seeks to overcome the deficiencies of classical theism with a new concept of God. In particular, he is concerned to "dehellenize" the Christian thought of God.

B. *The Death of God Controversy,* by Thomas W. Ogletree. Abingdon Press, 1966. 127 pp. An understanding account of the views of van Buren, Hamilton, and Altizer, with the author's own critical evaluation.

Notes

CHAPTER I
THE POLES OF THE DISCUSSION

1. Schubert M. Ogden, *The Reality of God* (Harper & Row Publishers, Inc., 1966), p. 14.

2. John Macquarrie, *Studies in Christian Existentialism* (The Westminster Press, 1966), pp. 5 f.

3. Harvey Cox, *The Secular City* (The Macmillan Company, 1965), p. 64.

4. James Alfred Martin, *The New Dialogue Between Philosophy and Theology* (The Seabury Press, Inc., 1966), p. 180.

5. John A. T. Robinson, *The New Reformation?* (The Westminster Press, 1965), p. 32.

6. Some of these books will be discussed in later chapters. All of them, together with other recent books of related interest, are listed with brief descriptive notes in the Appendix.

7. Macquarrie, *Studies in Christian Existentialism*, p. 10; also in *The Honest to God Debate*, ed. by D. L. Edwards (The Westminster Press, 1963), p. 187.

8. See below, pp. 43 ff.

9. Paul M. van Buren, *The Secular Meaning of the Gospel* (The Macmillan Company, 1963).

10. *Ibid.*, p. 133.

11. Ved Mehta, *The New Theologian* (Harper & Row, Publishers, Inc., 1966), p. 65.

12. Ronald Gregor Smith, *Secular Christianity* (London: William Collins Sons & Co., Ltd., 1966).

13. Van Buren, *The Secular Meaning of the Gospel*, pp. 57 ff.

14. R. Gregor Smith, *Secular Christianity,* p. 189.
15. See above, p. 16.
16. Eric Mascall, *The Secularization of Christianity* (London: Darton, Longman & Todd, Ltd., 1965).
17. *Ibid.,* p. 120.
18. *Ibid.,* p. 282.

CHAPTER II
THE THEOLOGICAL BACKGROUND

1. John Macquarrie, *An Existentialist Theology* (Harper & Row, Publishers, Inc., New Edition, 1965), p. 16, n. 23.
2. See above, p. 24.
3. Paul Tillich, *Systematic Theology,* Vol. I (The University of Chicago Press, 1951), p. 261.
4. Edwards, ed., *The Honest to God Debate,* p. 260.
5. Tillich, *Systematic Theology,* Vol. I, p. 14.
6. Nicolas Berdyaev, *The Beginning and the End,* tr. by R. M. French (Harper & Row, Publishers, Inc., 1957), p. 9.
7. See above, p. 16.
8. See below, pp. 59 ff.
9. Cf. my remarks in *The Scope of Demythologization* (Harper & Row, Publishers, Inc., 1960), Ch. I.
10. Rudolf Bultmann, *Jesus Christ and Mythology* (Charles Scribner's Sons, 1958), pp. 60 ff.
11. Helmut Gollwitzer, *The Existence of God as Confessed by Faith,* tr. by James W. Leitch (The Westminster Press, 1964), Part One.
12. See Herbert Braun, "The Problem of a New Testament Theology," in *The Bultmann School of Biblical Interpretation: New Directions?* ed. by Robert W. Funk, tr. by Jack Sanders (Harper & Row, Publishers, Inc., 1965), pp. 169 ff.
13. *Ibid.,* p. 183.
14. See especially Friedrich Gogarten, *Verhängnis und Hoffnung der Neuzeit. Die Säkularisierung als theologisches Problem* (Stuttgart: Friedrich Vorwerk Verlag, 1953). In English, there are available *Demythologizing and History,* tr. by Neville Horton Smith (London: SCM Press, Ltd., 1955), and *The Reality of Faith,* tr. by Carl Michalson et al. (The Westminster Press, 1959).
15. Carl F. von Weizsäcker, *The Relevance of Science* (London: William Collins Sons & Co., Ltd., 1964), pp. 157 ff.
16. Mehta, *The New Theologian,* p. 202.

17. Ogden, *The Reality of God,* p. 54.

18. Paul Lehmann, "Bonhoeffer: Real and Counterfeit," in *Union Seminary Quarterly Review,* Vol. XXI (March, 1966), pp. 364–365.

19. Karl Barth, *The Knowledge of God and the Service of God,* tr. by J. L. M. Haire and Ian Henderson (London: Hodder & Stoughton, Ltd., 1938), p. 21.

CHAPTER III
THE SECULAR OUTLOOK

1. The word translates *Geschichtlichkeit,* "historical existence."

2. See above, p. 20.

3. Cf. Martin Heidegger, "Die Zeit des Weltbildes," in *Holzwege* (Frankfurt-am-Main: Vittorio Klostermann, 1957), p. 69.

4. Hans Urs von Balthasar, *The God Question and Modern Man,* tr. by Hilda Graef (The Seabury Press, Inc., 1967), pp. 96–97.

5. See above, pp. 36–37.

6. Cox, *The Secular City,* pp. 21 ff.

7. C. E. Raven, *Natural Religion and Christian Theology,* Vol. I (London: Cambridge University Press, 1953), p. 54.

8. Martin Heidegger, *Über den Humanismus* (Frankfurt-am-Main: Vittorio Klostermann, 1947), p. 29.

9. Arend van Leeuwen, *Christianity in World History,* tr. by H. H. Hoskins (Charles Scribner's Sons, 1965).

10. Cf. Heinz R. Schlette, *Towards a Theology of Religions,* tr. by W. J. O'Hara (Herder & Herder, Inc., 1966).

11. Kenneth Cragg, "Encounter with Non-Christian Faiths," in *Union Seminary Quarterly Review,* Vol. XIX (May, 1964), p. 302.

12. *Ibid.,* p. 301.

CHAPTER IV
GOD IN THE WORLD

1. Arthur M. Ramsey, *Sacred and Secular* (Harper & Row, Publishers, Inc., 1965), p. 70.

2. See above, p. 31.

3. Cf. Tillich, *Systematic Theology,* Vol. I, p. 94.

4. Paul Tillich, *On the Boundary: An Autobiographical Sketch* (Charles Scribner's Sons, 1966), p. 13.

5. *The English Hymnal* (London: Oxford University Press, New Edition, 1933), Hymn 497: "There is a book who runs may read . . ."

6. *The English Hymnal,* Hymn 485: "Teach me, my God and King . . ."

7. See below, p. 111.

8. *"Haec omnia, Domine, semper bona creas, sanctificas, vivificas, benedicis et praestas nobis"* (from the Roman Missal).

9. H. C. N. Williams, *Coventry Cathedral* (London: Britannia Books, 1965), p. 29.

10. Karl Rahner, *The Church After the Council,* tr. by Davis C. Herron and Rodelinde Albrecht (Herder & Herder, Inc., 1966), p. 26.

11. See above, pp. 44 ff.

12. Dietrich Bonhoeffer, *Ethics,* tr. by Neville Horton Smith (London: SCM Press, Ltd., 1955), p. 61.

13. Arthur Vogel, *The Next Christian Epoch* (Harper & Row, Publishers, Inc., 1966), p. 77.

14. Alfred E. Taylor, *The Faith of a Moralist,* Vol. I (London: Macmillan & Co., Ltd., 1937), pp. 67 ff.

15. *Ibid.,* p. 95.

CHAPTER V

RELIGIONLESS CHRISTIANITY?

1. Thomas J. J. Altizer and William Hamilton, *Radical Theology and the Death of God* (The Bobbs-Merrill Company, Inc., 1966), pp. 39–40.

2. See above, p. 46.

3. See above, p. 41.

4. James Barr, *Old and New in Interpretation: A Study of the Two Testaments* (London: SCM Press, Ltd.; Harper & Row, Publishers, Inc., 1966), p. 29.

5. Cf. Martin Heidegger, *Being and Time,* tr. by J. Macquarrie and E. S. Robinson (London: SCM Press, Ltd.; Harper & Row, Publishers, Inc., 1962), p. 32.

6. Cf. Daisetz T. Suzuki, *An Introduction to Zen Buddhism* (London: Rider & Co., Publishers and Exporters, 1949), p. 124.

7. Frederick Herzog, *Understanding God* (Charles Scribner's Sons, 1966), pp. 117, 119.

8. Bonhoeffer, *Ethics*, p. 18.

9. This represented a modification of the earlier position of Kerrl, who had held that Christianity must be subordinate to the Nazi ideology. Cf. William L. Shirer, *The Rise and Fall of the Third Reich* (Crest Books, Fawcett Publications, Inc., 1962), p. 330.

10. Martin Thornton, *The Rock and the River* (London: Hodder & Stoughton, Ltd., 1965), p. 52.

CHAPTER VI

GOD AND CONTEMPORARY THOUGHT

1. See above, p. 47.

2. Thomas Aquinas, *Summa Theologiae*, Vol. I (London: Eyre & Spottiswoode Publishers, Ltd.; McGraw-Hill Book Company, Inc., 1964), p. 56.

3. Daniel Day Williams, "Christianity and Naturalism: An Informal Statement," in *Union Seminary Quarterly Review*, Vol. XII/4 (1957), p. 49.

4. John B. Cobb, Jr., *A Christian Natural Theology: Based on the Thought of Alfred North Whitehead* (The Westminster Press, 1965), p. 14.

5. Ogden, *The Reality of God*, pp. 56–57.

6. Williams, *loc. cit.*, p. 53.

7. Cf. my essay, "The Natural Theology of Teilhard de Chardin," in *Studies in Christian Existentialism*, pp. 183 ff.

8. Pierre Teilhard de Chardin, *Le Milieu Divin*, tr. by Bernard Wall and others (London: William Collins Sons & Co., Ltd., 1960).

9. See above, pp. 81–82.

10. Friedrich Gogarten, *Demythologizing and History*, tr. by Neville Horton Smith (London: SCM Press, Ltd., 1955), p. 52, n. 1.

11. Fritz Buri, *Theology of Existence*, tr. by H. H. Oliver and G. Onder (Attic Press, 1965), p. 30.

12. See above, pp. 34, 37.

13. See above, p. 32.

14. John Macquarrie, *Principles of Christian Theology* (Charles Scribner's Sons, 1966), especially Ch. V, pp. 94 ff.

15. Ian T. Ramsey, *Religious Language* (London: SCM Press, Ltd., 1957).

16. Mascall, *The Secularization of Christianity*, p. 8.

CHAPTER VII

THE REALITY OF GOD

1. See above, p. 48.

2. The fullest statement of his position is Thomas J. J. Altizer, *The Gospel of Christian Atheism* (The Westminster Press, 1966).

3. See the evaluations by Robert McAfee Brown in *Theology Today*, Vol. XXIII, No. 2 (July, 1966), pp. 279–290, and by T. W. Ogletree in *The Death of God Controversy* (Abingdon Press, 1966), pp. 75–108.

4. William Hamilton, *New Essence of Christianity* (Association Press, 1961; new edition with preface by Bishop Robinson, 1966).

5. *Ibid.*, p. 14.

6. J. Bright in *Peake's Commentary on the Bible*, ed. by Matthew Black and H. H. Rowley (New and rev. ed., London: Nelson & Sons, Ltd., 1962), p. 509.

7. Thomas J. J. Altizer and William Hamilton, *Radical Theology and the Death of God* (The Bobbs-Merrill Company, Inc., 1966), p. 28.

8. *Ibid.*, p. 44.

9. What I have called "faith in Being" is something like what Schubert Ogden means by "confidence in the final worth of our existence." Cf. Ogden, *The Reality of God*, p. 37.

10. John Courtney Murray, *The Problem of God: Yesterday and Today* (Yale University Press, 1964), p. 75.

11. Leslie Dewart, *The Future of Belief: Theism in a World Come of Age* (Herder & Herder, Inc., 1966), p. 207.

12. Jean Daniélou, *God and Us*, tr. by Walter Roberts (London: A. R. Mowbray & Company, Ltd., 1957), especially Ch. III, pp. 79 ff.

13. *Ibid.*, p. 105.

14. Dewart, *The Future of Belief*, p. 143.

15. Macquarrie, *Principles of Christian Theology*, pp. 179 ff.

CHAPTER VIII

THE DIVINE ATTRIBUTES

1. See above, pp. 100–101.

2. John M. E. McTaggart, *Some Dogmas of Religion* (London: Arnold & Sons, Ltd., 1906), pp. 186 ff.

3. Anselm, *Cur deus homo*, I, xii.

4. Cf. W. Eichrodt, *Theology of the Old Testament,* tr. by John Baker (London: SCM Press, Ltd., 1961), Vol. I, p. 181.

5. Macquarrie, *Principles of Christian Theology,* pp. 187 ff.

6. Rudolf Otto, *The Idea of the Holy,* tr. by J. W. Harvey (London: Oxford University Press, 1923), p. 14.

7. Martin Heidegger, *An Introduction to Metaphysics,* tr. by Ralph Manheim (Yale University Press, 1959), pp. 149–151.

8. Tillich, *Systematic Theology,* Vol. I, p. 211, etc.

9. Cf. my *Principles of Christian Theology,* pp. 310–312.

10. Cf. my *God-Talk* (Harper & Row, Publishers, Inc., 1967), especially Ch. X, "Analogy and Paradox," pp. 212 ff.

Chapter IX
God's Presence and Manifestation

1. John Bennett, "The Church and the Secular" in *Christianity and Crisis,* Vol. XXVI/22 (1966), p. 296.

2. See especially John Knox, *The Church and the Reality of Christ* (Harper & Row, Publishers, Inc., 1962).

3. See above, p. 131.

4. Martin Buber, *I and Thou,* tr. by R. Gregor Smith (2d ed., Edinburgh: T. & T. Clark, 1959), p. 75.

5. Dewart, *The Future of Belief,* p. 196.

Index

I. Subjects

Secularization, 36–37, 52, 88
Sin, 81
Social gospel, 25, 42
Sophists, 55
Subjectivism, 35
Supernaturalism, 34, 50, 77–78, 98, 118
Symbolism, 33, 119–120

Technology, 24, 43, 53, 54, 56–58, 69–70
Theism. *See* God
Theology: and culture, 61
and God, 13–15
history of, 52
natural, 40, 64, 86, 108
negative, 121–122

and philosophy, 92–101
pluralism in, 91
radical, 105
recent, 29–42
and secularity, 19–28, 131–138
status of, 47–48
Theonomy, 60
Transcendence, 21, 24–25, 28, 40, 49, 58, 65–66, 70, 98, 131, 134

Vocations, 69

World, 66–71, 132, 135
Worldliness, 66
Worship, 114

II. PERSONS

Alexander, Samuel, 92, 95
Altizer, Thomas J. J., 18, 22, 40, 105, 143, 148, 150
Anaxagoras, 54
Anselm, 118–119, 150
Aquinas, Thomas, 88–90, 149
Aristotle, 54, 89
Athanasius, 27

Balthasar, Hans Urs von, 51, 147
Barr, James, 56, 74, 148
Barth, Karl, 25, 28, 30, 39–41, 52, 56, 73–74, 129, 147
Bennett, John C., 131, 134, 151
Berdyaev, N., 33, 146
Bergson, Henri, 92, 93
Bethge, Eberhard, 38
Black, Matthew, 150

Bonhoeffer, Dietrich, 24, 30, 31, 37–39, 40, 66, 67, 82–84, 148, 149
Braun, Herbert, 35–36, 65, 97, 146
Bright, J., 150
Brown, R. M., 150
Brunner, Emil, 28
Buber, Martin, 137, 150
Buddha, 79
Bultmann, Rudolf, 23–24, 30, 34–36, 49, 97–98, 146
Buri, Fritz, 97, 149

Cobb, John B., 94, 142, 149
Cox, Harvey G., 16, 25–26, 27, 31, 36, 52–55, 142, 145, 147
Cragg, Kenneth, 58, 147

Daniélou, Jean, 112–113, 150

Rowley, H. H., 150

Sartre, Jean-Paul, 48, 96
Schlette, H. R., 57, 147
Schweitzer, Albert, 129
Shirer, William L., 149
Smith, Ronald Gregor, 23–25, 26, 31, 36, 37, 49, 143, 145, 146
Sophocles, 126
Spengler, Oswald, 56, 57
Starratt, Alfred B., 18, 141
Suzuki, D. T., 148

Taylor, A. E., 70–71, 148
Teilhard de Chardin, Pierre, 95–96, 149
Temple, William, 137
Thornton, Martin, 84, 142, 149
Thucydides, 55

Tillich, Paul, 16, 30, 31–33, 34, 59–61, 62, 98, 109, 123, 146, 147, 148, 151
Toynbee, Arnold, 56

Vahanian, Gabriel, 79, 140
van Buren, Paul, 21–23, 24, 25, 26, 27, 31, 40, 49, 140, 145
van Leeuwen, Arend, 56–58, 147
Vidler, Alex, 66
Vogel, Arthur, 70, 143, 148

Weiss, Paul, 18, 141
Weizsäcker, Carl F. von, 37, 146
Whitehead, Alfred North, 92, 93, 94
Williams, Daniel Day, 93, 94, 95, 149
Williams, H. C. N., 63, 148

III. SCRIPTURE REFERENCES

Main ~ *cultural* historical movements of Western culture → (The modern crises: main historical factors that have contributed to the *Secularisation* modern secular state).

1. The *glory that was Greece* πολις (modern secular state)
   - Science of democracy; the writings of Secularisation ← law (English) secular (scientific) history.
   - human motivation & this-worldly acts.

2. The Hebraic-Christian tradition.

3. The Reformation and the Renaissance
   - thro' the latter, science got going again (p.54)
     but had to fight a continual battle
     agst. theolog. prejudice fr. Galileo to
     Darwin. → The scientific method,
     → Scientific achievement,
   Autonomy of science, est. etc. liberation of fields of knowl. & esp. for domination of theology.

4. The Industrial Revolution.
   Beginnings of technology.

5. The Aufklärung

p. 52 - 56. On what factors have lead to
   Secularisation i.e. the secular outlook.